Perversions of the Market

SUNY series, Insinuations: Philosophy, Psychoanalysis, Literature

Charles Shepherdson, editor

Perversions of the Market
Sadism, Masochism, and the Culture of Capitalism

EUGENE W. HOLLAND

SUNY
PRESS

Avarice (*Avaritia*) from *The Seven Deadly Sins* (1558), engraving by Pieter van der Heyden (Netherlandish, ca. 1525–1569), The Metropolitan Museum of Art, New York, NY, courtesy of the Harris Brisbane Dick Fund, 1926. https://www.metmuseum.org/policies/frequently-asked-questions-image-and-data-resources.

Published by State University of New York Press, Albany

© 2024 State University of New York

All rights reserved

Printed in the United States of America

No part of this book may be used or reproduced in any manner whatsoever without written permission. No part of this book may be stored in a retrieval system or transmitted in any form or by any means including electronic, electrostatic, magnetic tape, mechanical, photocopying, recording, or otherwise without the prior permission in writing of the publisher.

Links to third-party websites are provided as a convenience and for informational purposes only. They do not constitute an endorsement or an approval of any of the products, services, or opinions of the organization, companies, or individuals. SUNY Press bears no responsibility for the accuracy, legality, or content of a URL, the external website, or for that of subsequent websites.

For information, contact State University of New York Press, Albany, NY
www.sunypress.edu

Library of Congress Cataloging-in-Publication Data

Name: Holland, Eugene W., author.
Title: Perversions of the market : sadism, masochism, and the culture of capitalism / Eugene W. Holland.
Description: Albany : State University of New York Press, [2024] | Series: SUNY series, Insinuations: Philosophy, Psychoanalysis, Literature | Includes bibliographical references and index.
Identifiers: ISBN 9798855800227 (hardcover : alk. paper) | ISBN 9798855800234 (ebook) | ISBN 9798855800210 (pbk. : alk. paper)
Further information is available at the Library of Congress.

This essay employs psychological categories because they have become political categories. The traditional borderlines between psychology on the one side and political and social philosophy on the other have been made obsolete by the condition of man in the present era: formerly autonomous and identifiable psychical processes are being absorbed by the function of the individual in the state—by his public existence. Psychological problems therefore turn into political problems: private disorder reflects more directly than before the disorder of the whole, and the cure of personal disorder depends more directly than before on the cure of the general disorder.

—Herbert Marcuse, *Eros and Civilization*

Contents

Preface		ix
Acknowledgments		xi

Part One: Historical

Introduction		1
Chapter One	Sadism and Masochism: The Sadism of Capitalist Production	11
Chapter Two	Borderline Conditions and Global Capitalism	31

Part Two: Theoretical

Introduction		59
Chapter Three	The Psychodynamics of the Capitalist Market	67
Chapter Four	The Sociodynamics of the Capitalist Market: Axiomatization	85
Conclusion		109
Notes		117
Works Cited		139
Index		151

Preface

The main point of this book is to show that capitalism fosters sadism and masochism—not as individual psychological proclivities but as widespread institutionalized patterns of behavior. There are of course many reasons, and at least as many ways, to condemn capitalism. Using the terms *sadism* and *masochism* to do so takes advantage of their manifestly negative connotations. It has the disadvantage of appearing to use psychological terms to diagnose a sociohistorical phenomenon. But that appearance is misleading. For one thing, psychological categories are something of an optical illusion: most of what appears to be psychological is in fact socioculturally overdetermined, with the notable exception of the physiological substrate of neuroplasticity, which is what opens "psychology" to social overdetermination in the first place. Brains in literate societies, to take just one example, are wired very differently from nonliterate brains (Henrich 2020). More importantly, the terms *sadism* and *masochism* were both derived from works of literature at the cost of ignoring almost everything that is literary about them, except their diagnostic power—which was aimed in the wrong direction. So here they will be rescued from their reductive appropriation for psychology and sexology and retooled to diagnose instead the nature of capitalist production and consumption, respectively. What I want to be able to say—and what I will in fact show in what follows—is that capitalist relations of production are *literally* sadistic and that capitalist relations of consumption are *literally* masochistic; and I mean "literally" here *literally*, provided we take the literary works after which these perversions were named at their word, and read them as diagnoses of capitalism rather than of individuals. Sadism and masochism will be shown to be perversions of the market in the sense that they are results of what capital does to markets. That diagnosis is the focus of chapter 1. But the classical perversions are not the only effect that capital has on markets. As the capitalist market becomes global in scale and drives production and consumption farther and farther apart, it fosters borderline conditions, which are based on psychic splitting rather than perversion. That diagnosis is the focus of chapter 2 and completes the historical part of the book.

The second part of the book is theoretical. The transformation of psychological terms into tools for sociohistorical analysis conducted here draws on well-known work by Herbert Marcuse (1955) and Norman O. Brown (1959), and on the ways they historicize psychoanalysis (Marcuse) and psychoanalyze history (Brown). But it also draws on the less-well-known work of Gilles Deleuze and Félix Guattari (1983, 1987, 1994) and their transformation of psychoanalysis into what they call "schizoanalysis." The point of part 2 is to explain the theoretical contributions schizoanalysis makes to the historical diagnoses of part 1; readers less interested in theory may skip right to the conclusion. Schizoanalysis shows first of all why it is so important to complement the analysis of family psychodynamics offered by Freud and the analysis of linguistic psychodynamics proposed by Lacan with an analysis of the psychodynamics of markets—particularly since Freud's Oedipus complex and death instinct are shown to be effects of capitalism (chapter 3). Second, schizoanalysis shows that once it has become the very basis of social organization, the capitalist market works as an open axiomatic system, based on abstract quantities (value) rather than meaningful codes, which has important implications for market psychodynamics (chapter 4). Last, schizoanalysis argues that the global market enhances the diagnostic power of thought in literature as well as philosophy, which explains why works by Sade and Masoch, but also Sartre and Camus and many others, can reveal so much about the perversion of the market by capital. They can also reveal the positive potential of markets as a basis for social organization, once freed from domination by capital—a subject touched on here but examined at length in my book *Nomad Citizenship* (Holland 2011).

My training in comparative literature took place mainly under the aegis of the "hermeneutics of suspicion," where literary works were treated as an expression of ideology to be unmasked or a symptom of some disorder to be diagnosed. So, my first book (1993), even though it showed how French poet Charles Baudelaire negotiated capital's "great transformation" of mid-nineteenth-century France into a market society by way of masochism and then borderline narcissism, treated him as a symptom rather than a diagnostician of culture. One aim of *Perversions of the Market*, although it does not do Baudelaire justice even in retrospect, is to restore to works of literature their ability to diagnose serious problems in contemporary social life as well as explore potential solutions to them.

Acknowledgments

I have a number of people to thank. The project first took shape under the supervision of Michel de Certeau, Fredric Jameson, Herbert Marcuse, and Richard Terdiman, with a grant from the French government for research in Paris, thanks to support from Jean-Joseph Goux and Luce Giard. It also benefited from a Mellon postdoctoral grant to take part in the Culture of Capital research program directed by Mark Fischer and George Marcus at Rice University. I am also grateful for the support of my Comparative Studies colleagues at Ohio State, especially chairs David Horn, Barry Shank, and Philip Armstrong. Conversations with Gilles Deleuze, William Connolly, and Kojin Karatani helped more than they could know. Special thanks to Brian Rotman, who among other things was the first to hear the project in its present form, and who seconded de Certeau's earlier recommendation to add a third term to the series containing sadism and masochism, in what would become the chapter on fascism and supremacisms. Eric Ball, Ron Bogue, Michael Ryan, and Dick Terdiman all provided invaluable feedback on early versions of the manuscript, and I am especially grateful to Rebecca Colesworthy at SUNY Press for her patience and skill in shepherding the book through the publication process and to her and series editor Charles Sheperdson for the very helpful feedback from the four anonymous reviewers they procured.

Special thanks, as always, to Eliza Segura for her insights, editorial expertise, patience, and support.

Portions of chapter 2 first appeared in "Schizoanalysis, Nomadology, Fascism," in *Deleuze and Politics*, ed. Thoburn and Buchanan (Edinburgh: Edinburgh University Press, 2008), 74–97, https://www.euppublishing.com.

Portions of the introduction to part 2 first appeared in "Utopian Thought in Deleuze and Guattari," in *Imagining the Future: Utopia and Dystopia*, ed. Milner, Ryan and Savage (Fitzroy, Victoria: Arena Publications, 2006), 217–42.

Part of chapter 3 first appeared in "Infinite Subjective Representation and the Perversion of Death," *Angelaki: Journal of the Theoretical Humanities* 5, no. 2 (2000): 85–91, reprinted by permission from Taylor & Francis, http://www.tandfonline.com

Portions of chapter 4 first appeared in "Multiplicities, Axiomatics, Politics," in *Deleuze, Guattari, and the Art of Multiplicity*, ed. Przedpelski and Wilmer (2020), 64–82, and in "Market Theory and Capitalist Axiomatics," *Deleuze and Guattari Studies* 13, no. 3 (2019): 309–30, both published by Edinburgh University Press, https://www.euppublishing.com.

Part One

Historical

Introduction

Sadism and masochism are better understood as perversions of the market by capital, rather than as perversions of individuals—although the perversions can indeed be personified in individuals both fictional and real. Achieving such an understanding will require rescuing these categories from psychological appropriations that have reduced complex works of literature by the Marquis de Sade (1740–1814) and Leopold von Sacher-Masoch (1836–1895) to simple expressions of a link between pleasure and pain and then turning them inside-out instead in order to diagnose historical moments in the development of capitalism that are also enduring aspects of the culture of capitalism. In order to redefine these categories, I draw on a number of post-Freudian psychoanalytic theorists—notably Herbert Marcuse, Norman O. Brown, and Gilles Deleuze and Felix Guattari. But in order to avoid an infantile determinism that construes childhood events as unilaterally determining later psychic complexes, I deploy an underused category championed by Freud himself—the concept of *Nachträglichkeit*, or deferred action (*après coup* in French)—according to which it is later events that retroactively confer meaning on earlier ones, rather than the other way around.[1]

Sade's and Masoch's literary works are thus to be considered not expressions of individual proclivities, but rather dramatizations of the links between pleasure, pain, and unevenly distributed power that characterize the basic social institutions and practices of capitalism. For dramatic effect, it is true, the literary works sexualize and personify these institutional practices in exaggerated form.² But to focus on dramatic technique would be to miss the important lessons these works have to teach us about capital—most notably, that it fosters the classic perversions known as "sadism" and "masochism."³ When a wise man points to the moon, as the saying goes, only a fool looks at the finger. I therefore need to draw distinctions among three sets of terms. I will in what follows retain the terms *sadism* and *masochism* in lowercase to designate what psychologists call "active" and "passive" algolagnia, respectively: the simple lived connection between pleasure and pain.⁴ *Sadism* and *Masochism* will be capitalized to refer to the diagnoses of the culture of Western capitalism made possible by comparing the very different literary forms of Sadean and Masochean discourse.⁵

Treating these literary works as diagnostic rather than expressive helps explain why Sade's oeuvre appeared nearly a century before Masoch's: Sadism corresponds to the emergence of capitalist production, while Masochism corresponds to a later moment when consumerism becomes essential to capitalism's survival and expansion.⁶ Of course, production and consumption remain key elements of the capitalist economy today, so Sadism and Masochism must be understood not only in relation to stages of capitalist development, but also as enduring features of capitalist culture.⁷ Yet capitalism undergoes a sea change in the course of its development. Before capitalism, production and consumption remained in relatively close proximity to one another, both geographically and morally. In subsistence economies, indeed, production and consumption practically coincide. The advent and expansion of trade, however, gradually separate production and consumption from one another, and capital accelerates the process immeasurably. As the mediation of accumulated capital and the world market drive production and consumption farther and farther apart geographically, the division of labor and increasing specialization make them incommensurable qualitatively, quantitatively, and morally: what someone produces has less and less bearing on what and how much they consume or can afford to consume. Of this momentous, world-historical process, what concerns us here is the disintegration or fragmentation of the psyche that results. Whereas Sadism and Masochism each provides a discrete and comprehensive diagnostic vantage point on the development of capitalist production and consumption across the eighteenth and nineteenth centuries, no such singular category (or author) can be found to diagnose capitalist culture in the twentieth century. What emerges instead is a welter of diagnostic categories—such as borderline conditions, schizophrenia, schizoaffective disorder, dissociative personality disorder, schizotypal personality, autism, narcissism, neurodiversity—and an equally wide range of literary and cinematic works, each of which provides insight into one or more aspects of advanced capitalist culture, yet without providing the kind of comprehensive vantage point presented by the works of Sade and Masoch. So, while chapter 1 takes the works of Sade and Masoch as its sole points of departure, chapter 2 draws on a disparate, yet far from exhaustive, set of novels and films for its diagnoses. That such a disparate set of narratives can be read to provide insights into advanced capitalist culture is itself testimony to the psychic fragmentation that culture has fostered.

Chapter 1 compares the ways that Sadism and Masochism are dramatized in Sade's and Masoch's works by contrasting the settings, the character types, the structure and dynamics of character interactions, the role of descriptions, and the narrative temporality that are typical of their literary works. Focusing on these literary features makes it possible to depersonify and depsychologize sadism and masochism and to construe the literary works instead as diagrams of the production and consumption relations lying at the heart of the capitalist economy. The psychic disintegration characteristic of twentieth-century culture, however, calls for different reading protocols. Following Freud's analysis of psychic defense mechanisms, second- and third-generation psychoanalysts noted a shift from neurosis and perversion, which fortify the ego, to very different defenses based on psychic splitting that weaken the ego and indeed border on psychosis, whence the umbrella term *borderline conditions*. Chapter 2, therefore, examines each work in a relatively large set of novels and films quite briefly, in order to assemble a mosaic of psychic disintegration and the varied and often diametrically opposed responses to it.

The increasingly remote and fraught relation between capitalist production and consumption turns out to be important for understanding not only the historical disintegration of the psyche, but also the cultural effects of capitalism's cyclical oscillations between moments of prosperity and liberal largesse, on one hand, and retrenchment and authoritarian austerity, on the other. In a previous work (Holland 1993), I examined an early instance of such oscillation as it registers in the writings of the great romantic-turned-modernist French poet Charles Baudelaire, when the utopian-socialist dreams of the Revolution of 1848 succumbed to the repressive authoritarianism of Napoleon III's Second Empire. And I suggested there that Baudelaire's experience subsequently found echoes in the life and writings of Walter Benjamin (1973)—who characterized Baudelaire as the lyric poet of high capitalism just as mid-twentieth-century Europe was succumbing to fascism—and in my own experience of post–World War II prosperity as it succumbed to the post-1968 oil crises and the rise of the anti-Keynesian, Christian-nationalist, white-supremacist Right, starting with the Reagan and Thatcher regimes and leading directly to the Trump presidency of 2017 through 2021. Here, I substantiate that suggestion by situating those cyclical oscillations in the wider historical context of "modernity," starting with the consolidation of European mercantile capitalism as it registers in literary and philosophical works of the sixteenth and seventeenth centuries, moving through the emergence of capitalist production and consumerism in the eighteenth and nineteenth centuries, respectively, and ending with the disintegration of the psyche characteristic of advanced capitalism in the twentieth century.

The use of psychological categories for sociohistorical analysis is by no means foreign to psychoanalysis, starting with Freud himself. For Freud, the key mechanism was *projection*: in *Totem and Taboo* (1953, vol. 13), for example, the intergenerational struggle for political power was modeled on the Oedipal rivalry between father and son for possession of the mother; despite the secular increase in repression over the millennia separating *Hamlet* from *Oedipus Rex*, *The Interpretation of Dreams* treats both plays as projections of the same psychic material: "the relation of the son to his parents" (1953, vol. 4, 83–86); in *Moses and Monotheism* (1953, vol. 23, 58), Freud insists that "religious phenomena are to be understood only on the pattern of the neurotic symptoms of the individual." In what follows, by contrast, sociohistorical factors take precedence over psychology: the key mechanism might be better called "introjection" rather than projection, were it not for the implication that the psyche could somehow be independent of sociohistorical forces to begin with.

Dramatic validation for such a reversal was provided by an experiment conducted at Stanford University by social psychologist Philip Zimbardo in 1971 (Haney 1973; Zimbardo 1973). Having converted part of a campus building into a mock prison, Zimbardo randomly assigned carefully screened student volunteers to the roles of prisoners and guards, in order to determine whether the brutality typical of prison guards was the expression of an innate psychological trait or a behavior induced by the institutional context. The student guards' behavior quickly became so viciously sadistic, and the student-prisoners' so abjectly submissive, that an experiment planned to last two weeks had to be terminated after just six days. The participants—who had shown no signs whatsoever of proclivities toward violence or servility in their screening tests—internalized the institutional roles and sadomasochistic behaviors governing prison life all too well. It may be only under conditions as artificial and extreme as these that it would appear that innate psychological disposition counts for nothing at all and that institutional setting determines practically everything. Nevertheless, the Zimbardo experiment confirms the importance of assigning social factors greater weight in the analysis of cultural artifacts and historical phenomena than orthodox Freudian psychoanalysis allows.

Some post-Freudian psychoanalysis, however, has incorporated social determinations into the analysis of the culture and history of capitalism. Wilhelm Reich (2000), for example, considered intrapsychic conflict and repression as internalized expressions of class conflict and political oppression. He understood the superego not primarily in terms of paternal or parental authority, as Freud did, but as a psychic representative of the ruling class. The drive for instinctual gratification is thus repressed, according to Reich, not in the name of incest taboos, family harmony, conscience, or civilized morality, but in the name of political inequality and for the sake of perpetuating class rule. Herbert Marcuse (1955), in turn, recast Reich's insights in terms of the economics rather than the politics of capitalist society, linking repression to economic exploitation rather than class domination. In Marcuse's view, social determinations must be added to Freud's concept of the reality principle as well as to his notion of repression in order for them to retain their critical force. For according to Freud, it is not only the demands of the superego that require repression, but the demands of reality itself. Particularly under conditions of scarcity, humans adopt the reality principle and moderate the drive for pleasure, repressing its insistence on immediate gratification for the sake of longer-term gains. But such repression is necessary only to the extent that so-called "reality" cannot satisfy our desires and hence requires us to delay gratification and devote ourselves to work. Yet the immense productivity of capitalism, Marcuse argues, has transformed that "reality" beyond recognition, virtually eliminating the conditions of scarcity that gave rise to the repressive reality principle when grueling labor may have been necessary just to survive. Yet even long after the conquest of scarcity, we are still repressed. And this, Marcuse suggests, is because under capitalism we operate not according to a reality principle—since the reality of capitalism is immense wealth and only the illusion of scarcity—but rather according to what he calls the "performance principle." And this performance principle requires not just repression, but surplus repression: we work far more than "reality" itself would require. To the extent that the economy functions to produce surplus value to be privately appropriated by capitalists instead of producing wealth to be collectively enjoyed by all, we suffer from surplus repression rather than repression tout court.

As valuable as the insights of Reich and Marcuse may be, they share one singular disadvantage: they dilute what is probably the cornerstone of psychoanalytic theory—the concept of unconscious repression. Delaying gratification by working to obtain something that is not immediately available from "reality" isn't (usually) an unconscious act; but repression in the sense psychoanalysis gives to the term requires not only that an original drive (e.g., for immediate gratification) be excluded from consciousness, but that the act of exclusion itself be repressed and remain unconscious along with the drive. As apt a descriptive term as the performance principle may be, there are probably very few people who are unaware of what they are doing when they go to work, and such unawareness could as likely be attributed to ignorance as to actual repression in the psychoanalytic sense. Here is where the perspective of Marcuse's contemporary, Norman O. Brown, proves invaluable.

For Brown (1959) proposes a properly psychoanalytic explanation of what Marcuse calls "surplus repression" and the performance principle, based on a repressed infantile complex that becomes an enduring unconscious motivation throughout adulthood. Human beings are destined to perform relentlessly in excess of real needs, according to Brown, because of the peculiar nature of human infancy. Human children's prolonged dependence on parental care giving and the intense, effortless gratification resulting from that care together create unrealistic expectations of future gratification—expectations that parents and reality inevitably disappoint as the child matures. Such disappointment breeds angry resentment of the parents for failing to provide gratification, yet the infant remains dependent on them for its very survival. Capable of renouncing neither their expectations nor their parental bonds, physiologically and emotionally dependent on parents and unable to accept separation from them (which during the formative years would mean death), children develop a complex that Freud referred to as "separation anxiety." In Brown's view, however, this complex involves far more than just anxiety over separation from parents: it is based on the repression of the death instinct, in two related but conflicting ways. On one hand, children cling to infantile expectations of immediate and infinite gratification, refusing in effect to let unrealistic expectations die a natural death. On the other hand, children accept a life of dependency with parents rather than death without them, turning their resentment of parental disappointment inward as guilt. Then as the maturing child eventually adopts the reality principle in the face of inevitable disappointment, the entire complex gets repressed.

But repression, of course, is only a partial solution at best for, as Freud insisted, a repressed drive never gives up: it persistently strives to repeat the original experience of satisfaction. All that repression accomplishes is to redirect the instinctual drive away from its now-impossible original aim in the direction of substitute gratifications. But since as substitutes they can never satisfy the drive, instinctual tension persists, fueling the repetition compulsion. For the rest of its life, the child will be compelled to search endlessly for more substitutes, none of which will reproduce the original experience of effortless, immediate, and complete gratification. This compulsion to repeat generates what Brown calls a neurotic form of history—known colloquially as "progress"—in which fixation on the infantile past produces an unconscious and futile quest to repeat that past in the future. For Brown, then, Marcuse's performance principle has its origins in the separation-anxiety characteristic of human infancy. Separation anxiety generates a repetition compulsion to recreate the conditions of infantile gratification through ever-increasing levels of consumption and production.

As compelling as Brown's account of "the psychoanalytical meaning of history" is, by placing the nature of human infancy and ensuing separation-anxiety at the center of his explanation of history, he has clearly reverted to the psychologism inherent in orthodox Freudian theory, favoring projection over introjection. Indeed, this is his explicit intention: to replace "external," and especially Marxist, explanations for political domination and economic exploitation with an "internal," psychological explanation. But in doing so, Brown has left out of account another key Freudian concept: *Nachträglichkeit*, or deferred action. On this view, events and experiences can acquire meaning *nachträglich*, after the fact. This being so, what I want to argue is that however traumatic the separation complex may or may not be in childhood, it must be said that capital reproduces and exacerbates separation anxiety and the ensuing compulsion to repeat on a society-wide and now global scale. Just as childhood combines the effortless luxury of parents' affection and sustenance with absolute dependence on them and the ever-growing threat of separation from them, capital produces immeasurable wealth while reducing the vast majority of us to absolute dependence on it for our livelihood and subjects us to the ever-present threat (if not the actual experience) of destitution. In the capitalist economy, everyone who sells their labor power on the market in exchange for a wage with which to buy back the means of life (food, shelter, and so forth) necessarily faces destitution, and by implication, death, once they are separated from the means of production by losing their job—or indeed by not getting one in the first place. Under capitalism, in other words, infantile separation anxiety is not resolved or mitigated in adult life, but rather reproduced and intensified.

Such "primitive dispossession"—namely, the condition of being separated from the means of life—is a basic and necessary feature of capitalism, a corollary of the process of "so-called primitive accumulation" essential to the emergence and on-going expansion of the capitalist economy. While "primitive accumulation" refers to the process whereby means of production come to be owned privately (become capital) rather than shared for the common good, "primitive dispossession" results in the necessity of selling one's labor power to private owners of capital once separated from means of life that are no longer held in common. The Enclosure Acts in sixteenth-century Britain are a classic illustration of this process of separation in its early stages. In connection with a growing protocapitalist textile industry, the Enclosure Acts appropriated for sheep-grazing land that had been used for crops or held in common. The result was that a vast population that had been securely (if oppressively) tied to the land was now cut off from its traditional means of subsistence and would soon become dependent on an emerging job market to earn wages to buy food.[8] Henceforth the capitalist market stands between people and their means of life: for those fortunate to have a job and earn money, the market mediates connection with a variety of goods; for those without jobs and without sufficient purchasing power, however, the market becomes a barrier that actually precludes access to the means of life. Under capitalism, then, the necessity of selling one's labor power to buy back means of life and the resulting separation anxiety that results have become a general condition of existence.

Now the point of showing separation anxiety to be a basic feature of capitalist society is that widespread separation anxiety produces a culture dominated by the repetition compulsion, and the compulsion to repeat lies at the heart of both Sadism and Masochism. Ordinarily, we repeat what we have found pleasurable in the past in order to obtain pleasure again in the future: repetition serves the pleasure principle. But in perversion (as in neurosis more generally), the compulsion to repeat becomes so strong that it actually takes precedence over the pleasure principle: in Sadism and Masochism, repetition governs pleasure, actually determines what is sought out as pleasurable, rather than the other way around—to the point of making even pain into something desirable. In Freud's simplest, dynamic model of the pleasure principle, pleasure occurs when an increase in tension is followed by a release of tension. Masochism repeats the increase of tension to obtain perverse pleasure in suffering pain; Sadism perversely repeats the release of tension in inflicting pain. And that is one reason why they are best understood as specifically capitalist perversions: they belong to (and can help diagnose) a culture in which the compulsion to repeat has taken precedence over the pleasures of enjoyment. Adducing additional reasons tying Sadism to capitalist production and Masochism to capitalist consumption (consumerism) will require closer examination of the narrative structure and dynamics of Sade's and Masoch's literary works in their respective cultural contexts.

Chapter One

Sadism and Masochism

The Sadism of Capitalist Production

In order to recognize the diagnostic force of Sade's work, we have to understand how it functions textually. Sadean discourse draws on three main precursors from early modernity: Luther, Machiavelli, and More. Luther's Protestant Reformation rejected worldly good works as a path to salvation in favor of an abstract, other-worldly principle of faith. Personal devotion to an inner spiritual life counted for more than the outward results of such a life, which were considered unreliable at best, if not indeed misleading. Salvation is to be achieved solely "through the redemption that is in Christ Jesus. . . . and cannot be otherwise acquired or grasped by any work, law, or merit."[1] Max Weber (1958) would, of course, link the later, Calvinist emphasis on work and asceticism directly to the emergence of capitalism, but Luther's initial insistence on salvation through inner faith alone and the corollary dismissal of worldly good works introduces a radical split between inner and outer life, between ideal and real, that will resonate with other modern thinkers up to and including Sade. Ironically enough, despite being a virulent critic of nascent capitalism, Luther nonetheless thereby contributes to a form of thought wholly conducive to capitalist production.

Machiavelli (1968) casts the split between ideal and real in very different terms, where what is at issue is not faith and salvation, but reason and power. The prince must also abandon the aim of doing worldly good, but he does so in order to establish and maintain his grasp on power. Whereas classical philosophy and Christian theology had tried to assure that reason and the good would remain aligned with one another, Machiavelli severs substantive rationality tied to the good from formal rationality (to adopt Weber's terms) and subordinates the former to the latter. For Machiavelli, *virtu* is the flexible exercise of reason in the service of power, particularly with the aim of subduing *fortuna*—the hazards and threats of unpredictable Nature and humanity. The Machiavellian exercise of reason utterly independently of any concern for doing good is just one step shy of exercising reason for the sake of doing bad—and this is the step Sade takes by drawing on the utopian genre initiated by Thomas More (2002).

Three features of the utopian genre are crucial, and they all involve the relation of utopia to satire (Elliott 1972). First of all, utopia can be considered a philosophical genre in that it is based on the exchange of ideas. More's main characters, Raphael and Hythloday, for example, engage in long discussions about the state of English society and the ideas behind the society of Utopia. Indeed, all utopias mobilize some kind of plot mechanism to justify long excursuses explaining the rationale for their versions of utopian society—often the arrival of a visitor who wants or needs to be shown how the society works. Mennipean satire is the subgenre of satire that places this philosophical aspect of the utopian genre center stage: Mennipean satire presents a set of diverse ideas by staging a discussion among a number of characters who are little more than mouthpieces for the ideas under consideration. Utopia in effect reduces this number to two: the ignorant visitor, representing the ideas and norms of existing society, and the utopian tour guide, representing the superior ideas and norms of the ideal, utopian society.

Second, utopia reverses the relation between the real and the ideal that characterizes satire. The main thrust of satire is to present a critique of existing society; the ideals on which this critique is based remain implicit. The main thrust of utopia, conversely, is to present the rationale for an ideal society through its depiction in fictional form; the critique of real society remains implicit. More's inaugural utopia illustrates this reversal perfectly. Book 1 of *Utopia* is a free-wheeling discussion focused primarily on criticizing the ills of existing English society; the ideals on which the critique is based remain implicit. The function of book 2 is to make those ideals explicit, through Raphael's depiction of Utopia and his justifications for its salient features. As the genre evolves, the satirical moment becomes almost entirely implicit, and the depiction of and rationale for the ideal society come to predominate.

Third, as utopia and satire diverge in the course of their historical development, not only does the gap separating ideal and real, positive and negative, become more and more pronounced, but satire itself loses its earlier ambivalence. Premodern satire operated under the sign of Saturn—a two-faced god more or less evenly balancing the good and the bad—drawing on the body to deflate the arrogance of abstract ideas and drawing on ideas to mitigate the flaws and absurdities of embodied human existence (Bakhtin 1968). With the advent of modernity, this ambivalence gives way to pure negativity, as the body is increasingly used in satire to viciously and unrelentingly excoriate its real objects, while utopia presents the ideal in purer and purer, albeit purely fictional, forms.

In this context, Sadean discourse performs something of a reversal of the reversal or a union of opposites in relation to satire and utopia. The Sadean ideal is depicted in fictional form and rationalized in long excursuses by various characters—as in the utopian genre (and Menippean satire)—and the body has become an object and source of pure derision and pain—as in modern satire. Indeed, sodomy is the ideal Sadean sex act because it represents sterility and subjugation completely devoid of mutual pleasure or potential for reproduction.[2] Following Machiavelli, rationality is divorced from the good; in Sade, reason is mobilized not for the sake of doing good but for the sole purpose of justifying the exercise of power and the infliction of bodily pain. However, true to the utopian genre of which it must be considered a perverse variant, Sadean discourse leaves the real object of its critique implicit. One of the aims of this chapter is to make explicit what the object of Sadean critique actually is.

In *Dialectic of Enlightenment*, drawing on Nietzsche's critique of Kant, Horkheimer and Adorno (1972) have already shown that Sade can be understood as a critic of "enlightened thought . . . [and] the social institutions with which it is interwoven" (xiii) and of "Western bourgeois civilization" and its "blind domination" of nature more generally (xvi). They support their argument very effectively by quoting extensively from the philosophical excursuses of a plethora of Sadean characters, including Francavilla (87–89, 95–96), Juliette (95–97, 104), Clairwil (96, 101–2) and others. While there is nothing wrong with this approach or Horkheimer and Adorno's conclusion, an examination of the literary form of Sade's works rather than just characters' opinions will enable us to identify the object of Sadean critique more precisely: capitalist production relations.

Freed from the reductive symmetry of psychologized sadomasochism, Sadean and Masochean discourse can be compared to highlight the very different literary forms taken by Sadism and Masochism in their literary works (Deleuze 1971). The Sadists' program of systematically abusing other people psychologically and sexually takes place in an institutional context, diametrically opposed to the domestic setting of Masochism. The Sadistic institution is governed by rules expounded and rationalized at great length in the philosophical excursuses of prominent characters, whereas character interactions in the Masochistic domestic sphere are governed by contract. Character interactions in Sade's institutions are structured by a stark division between those exhibiting an inferior, sentimental, "secondary" nature and those possessing a superior, rational, "primary" nature. Among Sade's principal targets here is the naive sentimentality of Rousseau's "natural man."[3] In psychoanalytic terms, the superior characters identify with the superego and project the ego onto the victims they torture. The action of Sade's narratives consists of an endless accumulation of violent punishments repeatedly inflicted by the former on the latter, undertaken in the name of a cold and utterly dispassionate rationality, and interrupted frequently by expositions of the principles of Sadism. Masoch's narratives, by contrast, are so full of suspense that there is almost no action at all. The issue then becomes what even such a brief examination of literary form can tell us about the object of Sadean critique.

Adorno and Horkheimer are right to see Sade's highly regimented orgies as parodies of the modern, means-ends rationality inaugurated by Machiavelli and perfected by Kant: focused on means, "reason [as] the organ of calculation [and] planning . . . is neutral in regard to ends" (88). Yet Sade's libertines relish and extol more than the Machiavellian exercise of power for its own sake: their gratification comes specifically from the pain and humiliation inflicted on their subjugated victims. And in this respect, they are following Kant's categorical imperative to the letter. For "acting only when the maxim of action can be considered a universal law," as prescribed by Kant, can result in suffering and even death, as real consequences get sacrificed to the ideal of abstract rationality. Take the classic case of an abolitionist hiding runaway slaves in the basement: when the slave owner knocks on the door and asks if his slaves are there, the categorical imperative forbids the abolitionist from lying to protect them, even though he knows they will suffer corporal punishment (or worse) as a result. Sade, it is true, sexualizes this interpersonal dynamic for dramatic effect, but the pattern is the same: those acting in accordance with the formal rationality of the categorical imperative can end up inflicting pain on others.

A similar pattern reappears in Kant's discussion of the sublime (Kant 2007, §§ 24–28), again echoing Machiavelli and developing features of the struggle of the power of reason (*virtu*) against the vagaries of Nature (*fortuna*). In what we can call the contingent sublime (which Kant calls the dynamical sublime), we are able to enjoy the sight of an otherwise terrifying natural phenomenon (a volcano, a hurricane) as long we are not in fact endangered by it. The mind is able to rise above the natural phenomenon because, given the circumstances, it knows its existence is not threatened. In what we can call the "absolute sublime" (which Kant tellingly calls the "mathematical sublime"), perception is overwhelmed by an object so large as to defy measurement, but the rational mind has recourse to the idea of infinity, which designates an absolute totality larger than any real object. Regardless of circumstances, Kant insists, "It is . . . for us a law (of reason) . . . that we should esteem as small in comparison with ideas of reason [namely, the idea of infinity] everything which for us is great in nature as an object of sense" (§ 27). In both of its forms, then, the experience of the sublime for Kant amounts to the feeling of the superiority of reason's power over nature.[4]

This recourse of the rational mind to mathematics in order to dominate nature is indeed characteristic not just of Kantian ethics and aesthetics, but of Enlightenment epistemology and technology more generally. Breaking with the reigning Aristotelianism, Galileo set out to develop a universal theory that construed all matter and motion as subject to mathematical description and prediction. Descartes famously introduced the distinction between *res cogitans* (mind) and *res extensa* (matter), arguing that humanity could thereby "make [themselves] as it were the masters and possessors of nature" (2006, 51). Locke would then translate Descartes's mind/body dualism into the distinction between absolute primary qualities, which define reality as essentially mathematical in nature, and contingent secondary qualities, which describe how that reality is perceived by embodied humans. Colors, according to this distinction, are really determined by wavelengths of light, colors' primary qualities; what we perceive and what we call them are secondary qualities, dependent on human physiology and the cultures to which we belong. The use of mathematics to dominate nature then becomes a veritable program with Francis Bacon (2000). Scientific knowledge, as Horkheimer and Adorno point out, becomes the exercise of power over nature. Indeed, Bacon (2002) expresses his disdain for any knowledge not used to dominate nature in terms that prefigure Sade's preference for sodomy as the ultimate act of sexual domination: "Knowledge that tendeth [not to operation (*scientia operativa*)] but to satisfaction, is but as a courtesan, which is for pleasure, and not for fruit or generation."[5] But Bacon's program entailed more than the use of mathematics to dominate nature. He recommended sending agents around to workshops to collect the practical know-how embodied in artisans' skills; that know-how would be transformed into abstract scientific knowledge in the laboratory and then reapplied to production processes to improve efficiency and increase output. Separating conception from execution in this way would introduce a novel form of labor domination: workers would henceforth be told by "management" precisely how to do the work; and eventually, enhancing the production process through the introduction of technology would eclipse lengthening the working day as the primary means of assuring profitable returns on capital investment. This subordination of the work process to scientific abstraction, technological innovation, and formal management is just as important a feature of Bacon's program as the subordination of nature itself to science for which Bacon is better known.

Of course, managing the labor process in this way depends on the momentous historical shift from selling just the products of labor as commodities on the market to selling labor power itself as a commodity on the job market, one of the mainstays of capitalist production. Although not yet the dominant form of labor, wage labor was widely identified and critiqued as a form of slavery throughout eighteenth-century Europe.[6] With the commodification of labor power, remuneration for work is no longer based on the amount or quality of the goods produced, but on the amount of time spent working to produce them. It is primarily for this reason that applying technology to the work process can increase the amount of goods produced without increasing the amount paid to the workers producing them. Henceforth the concrete use value or material quality of the work counts for less than its abstract exchange value as measured by the quantity of time spent working.

A similar process of dematerialization affects money, another mainstay of capitalist relations of production. The first step in this process was taken in the early decades of the seventeenth century by mercantalist city-states such as Amsterdam, Florence, and Venice, with the introduction of the banknote (e.g., the *Marc Banco*, the *Florin de Banque*). It had two salient features. First of all, its value did not depend on its actually containing a quantity of precious metal, the way contemporary coinage did. Its value was immaterial, purely nominal, and thus did not suffer from debasement or clipping. But the banknote was not designed to circulate freely (although it increasingly did so as the century wore on): it was in effect a contract between the state bank and a specific individual named on the banknote, whereby the former would pay the designated amount to the latter upon demand. By the end of the century, however, the invention of paper money removed this contractual limitation, as the name of a specific individual was replaced by "the bearer;" paper money could now circulate freely. It had become an institution: its value was determined not materially, but purely by convention. And its superiority to specie was twofold: its nominal value would never diminish from debasement or clipping, no matter how widely it circulated, and it could be created at will by state banks without direct recourse to scarce precious metals.[7]

A similar transformation takes place, finally, in mathematics in the early modern period (Rotman 2000). Mathematical notation grows more abstract and immaterial even as it supports more and more complicated types of calculation. Primitive mathematical (or protomathematical) notation is directly material and iconic: one physical counter or graphic mark is used to designate each counted item—a system that soon becomes nearly impossible to work with. Roman numerals (among many other systems of notation) offered a partial solution: tens, hundreds, and thousands would each be given a different, arbitrary mark, so that one *M*, for example, would replace a thousand individual marks. But four thousand still requires four *M*s, ten thousand requires ten *M*s, a hundred thousand would require one hundred *M*s, and so on. Roman notation thus only partially (for numbers under one thousand) exempted itself from having to physically reiterate iconic marks for large numbers. Moreover, Roman notation was impractical if not impossible to use for calculation.[8] So given the growing importance of trade and technology, by the beginning of the seventeenth century, so-called Arabic (but in fact originally Hindu) notation had replaced Roman numerals throughout Europe. Arabic notation not only facilitated calculation and enabled double-entry bookkeeping, but its decimal-place system made it feasible to write large numbers practically without iconic reiteration. To the already considerable power of Arabic notation, a series of European mathematicians added exponentiation, which made writing increasingly large (and increasingly small) numbers even easier: the sequence of zeroes in the decimal-place system was replaced by a single (positive or negative) number in superscript.[9] The size of the number now bore practically no relation to the length of the numeral representing it—a process culminating with the adoption in the midseventeenth century of a single symbol, ∞, to designate infinity. A quantity not just impractical but literally impossible to represent iconically could now be represented symbolically and enter into calculations with the stroke of a quill. Compared with the materiality of iconic marks, mathematical notation had practically freed itself from iconicity altogether and become abstract and purely conventional. And infinity, which had long been attributed as a physical and/or moral attribute to the cosmos or

God, or treated as a paradox in Greek philosophy, now becomes an issue of calculation, most notably with the development toward the end of the seventeenth century of infinitesimal calculus.

In all these instances, a specific form of instrumental rationality—abstract, ideal, quantitative, calculable—prevails over real consequences (Kant), qualitative sense experience and emotion (Descartes, Locke, Kant), artisanal know-how and practices (Bacon), in much the same way that Sade's libertines, albeit more dramatically, subject their victims to endless rounds of sexualized abuse in the name of pure reason. Galilean-Lockean epistemology with its distinction between primary and secondary qualities enables enhanced treatment of raw materials in the production process. The development of metrical land surveys grounds bourgeois property rights just as the development of planetary cartography based on functional longitude as well as latitude (dating from 1530) facilitates planetary navigation in the service of empire (Moore 2023). Replacing Roman with Arabic/Hindu numerals and the decimal-place system, combined with the Baconian translation of artisinal know-how into abstract scientific knowledge, bolsters the development of technology to further enhance the efficiency of the production process. And the application of technology to the production process in turn makes the workforce subordinate to management. The Kantian categorical imperative, meanwhile, facilitates the management of the workforce by stipulating an abstract duty to respect the terms of contracts regardless of consequences, which would prove deleterious to the workers themselves. The dematerialization of money and the conversion of moral, cosmological, and paradoxical notions of infinity to a mathematical conception susceptible to calculation, finally, make the prospect of endless growth and accumulation readily conceivable, if not ultimately practicable. The result of the convergence of these instances is the treatment of both natural and human resources as quantified factors of production and the subordination of production, exchange, and consumption to the endless accumulation of surplus value.[10]

The distinction central to the institution of Sadism between primary and secondary character types thus ultimately points to the distinction between two types of private property and two very different objectives for production. On one hand, there is property in means of production that get advanced as capital to be used collectively by workers and management in production. On the other hand, there is property in the goods that get sold and bought on retail markets for the sake of private consumption. This distinction in turn reflects an ambivalence specific to capitalist production:

it aims to simultaneously produce wealth to be consumed and produce surplus value to be accumulated. But for capital, crucially, accumulating surplus value is the primary objective, while the enjoyment of wealth is strictly secondary, reduced in the interest of maximizing profit to the barest minimum made possible by the power capital wields over society at any given place and time (Nitzan and Bichler 2009). Note that this subordination of material wealth and enjoyment to abstract value and endless accumulation is specific to capitalist production: simple production for the market still aims at the enjoyment of wealth, even though the goods consumed are produced by trading partners rather than the consumers themselves (as they are in subsistence economies). It is the intervention of the "middle man," in both mercantile and full-fledged capitalism, that turns production away from—that is to say, perverts—the production and enjoyment of material wealth and subordinates them to the endless accumulation of abstract value.[11] This perversion of production leads in turn to a perversion of consumption: once surplus value takes precedence over value and wealth, consumption itself becomes a key factor in the accumulation of surplus value, henceforth subject to Sadistic practices such as predatory marketing and subprime lending. In addition to remaining a means of reproducing labor power, consumption becomes what is called the "realization" of surplus value in liquid form: transforming material goods which are themselves of no practical value to the capitalist back into money for further reinvestment. In this context, focusing exclusively on the sexualized dramas in Sade is like looking at the wise man's finger instead of the moon: reading his work diagnostically, by contrast, enables us to identify capitalist production as Sadistic, just as reading Masoch diagnostically will enable us to identify capitalist consumption as Masochistic.

It is one thing to show that capitalist production is Sadistic. But that raises the question of whether individual capitalists can be considered Sadists. Probably not in the narrow sexual sense, as Sade's characters are. But can they be considered social or "moral sadists"—akin to Freud's "moral masochists" who repeatedly engage in self-defeating or self-destructive behavior without deriving sexual gratification from it—that is to say, individuals who take satisfaction in inflicting pain or hardship on others without deriving explicitly sexual gratification from doing so? It is clear, for example, that many of the laws and policies crucial to the emergence of capitalism in England in the eighteenth century were Sadistic in the proper social-diagnostic sense of the term: they transformed peasants into factors of production by depriving them of access to their traditional means of life and forcing them to sell their labor power for wages (Perelman 2000; Polanyi 1944). But what about the attitude of one Arthur Young, who insisted at the time that "the lower classes must be kept poor, or they will never be industrious" (cited in Thompson 1963, 358)? Or the stance of John Arbuthnot, a contemporary of Young who argued in defense of the Enclosure Acts (1773) that "by converting the little farmers into a body of men who must work for others [by enclosing the commons] more labor is produced, . . . an advantage which the nation should wish for" (Arbuthnot 1773, 124)? The same sentiment echoed centuries later during the Reagan years, when George Gilder (1981) proclaimed that "In order to succeed, the poor need most of all the spur of poverty." Or take current US unemployment policy, which in order to ward off inflation that would devalue privately owned assets sets an "acceptable" unemployment target at around 2 percent, thereby depriving millions of citizens of access to the means of life: it is clearly Sadistic. But couldn't the same be said of the attitude of former Federal Reserve chairman Paul Volcker, who on the eve of announcing an interest-rate hike to curb inflation asked the *Wall Street Journal* whether he could count on their support "when there's blood all over the floor" as a result of the rate hike?[12] (A deputy *Wall Street Journal* editor [Melloan 2003] subsequently identified "Latin borrowers and American farmers" as the principal victims.) And what about Texas governor Abbott's ruling to deny employees working outside in extreme heat their right to water breaks (Singh 2023)? And what if not Sadistic is the glee with which Enron energy traders joked about "sticking it to Grandma Millie" after engineering electricity rate hikes of 250 percent or more for California consumers?[13] Even if calling these people themselves Sadists may seem somewhat extreme, calling their behaviors Sadistic seems eminently reasonable and justifiable given the proper understanding of Sadism.[14]

In any case, using Sadean discourse as a diagnostic tool reveals the early-modern innovations in ethics, aesthetics, epistemology, cartography, technology, and mathematics examined above to be among the real conditions that enabled the emergence and consolidation of capitalist production; they are not causes, but rather contributing factors.[15] To be clear: I am not claiming that these forms of thought, discourse, and practice caused capitalism to emerge, nor that nascent capitalism caused them to arise. They are enabling conditions rather than causes. In much the same spirit, Max Weber (1958) insisted that his examination of the relation between Protestant asceticism and capitalism was not intended "to substitute for a one-sided materialistic an equally one-sided spiritualistic causal interpretation of culture and of history," but rather to add "ascetic Protestantism in its relation to the other plastic elements of modern culture. . . . [and] the totality of social conditions" (183) as just one factor among many contributing to the rise of capitalism.[16] Indeed, it is important to include the Calvinist work ethic analyzed by Weber as itself an internalized personification of the programmatic Sadism of capitalist production, albeit without Sade's sexual dramatization: it entails the repudiation of sentiment and enjoyment not in others but in oneself, resulting in the endless accumulation of wealth.[17]

Recognizing the Sadism of Weber's Protestant work ethic is important because of the way that ethos has been weaponized in neoliberalism, arguably the dominant form of capitalism today—and by far the most dangerous.[18] Like the earlier work ethic, neoliberalism enjoins everyone to treat themselves as factors of production, to become "entrepreneurs of the self," as Foucault (2004a) put it. But the differences between the two are for my purposes equally important: the Calvinist work ethic was originally a belief system largely independent of contemporary systems of governance; its relations to capitalism and Sadism were unintentional, if not indeed unconscious. Neoliberalism, by contrast, was intentionally and explicitly formulated and implemented top-down as policy in response to (among other things) Keynesianism and late-twentieth-century crises of capital accumulation. Expanding on Foucault's lectures on the birth of neoliberalism, Wendy Brown (2015, 59) explains, "For Foucault, neo-liberalism was born not from crises of capitalist accumulation, as David Harvey and other Marxists would have it, but of liberal governmentality . . . [crises] gestated by Keynesianism, fascism, Nazism, state planning, and social democracy"—but of course it could be considered a response to both. And if it is indeed the case that the legitimacy of the liberal state is determined by the health of the economy, as Foucault and Brown suggest, then crises of liberal governmentality and crises of capitalist accumulation would amount to the same thing, as ruling elites try to restore growth and profit margins to a faltering economy by the imposition of austerity and a turn to financialization (Brown 2015; Harvey 2005b; Foucault 2004a).

Understanding this shift from ethic to policy, from belief to obedience, is of paramount importance. Agreeing with Marx, Weber foresaw that once established, capitalism would no longer need the support of religious ethics at all.[19] One might also adduce the growth of income inequality and the degradation of work itself as factors contributing to the shift from belief to obedience (Graeber 2019). Once pious belief in the American dream that hard work would pay off for everyone is shattered, it is no wonder people turn cynical about it and resent the authority of a state that exacts compliance with the intensified neoliberal version of it. But most important for my purposes is the way capital's imperative to increase consumption in order to forestall its inevitable crises of overproduction (a.k.a. underconsumption) undermines the ascetic work ethic of Calvinist Protestantism, and may even have replaced it. And in this connection, it is worth noting that not only was ascetic Protestantism just one of many factors conducive to the emergence of capitalist production relations, but Lutheran Calvinist Protestantism was just one of several strains of emergent Protestantism, many of which are missing from Weber's account altogether. In fact, Weber's Calvinist work ethic contrasts sharply with another major strain of Protestantism, which runs from Pietism through Sentimentalism to inform the Romantic movement. And the consumer ethic emerging from these strains of Protestantism will be among the key targets of Masoch's post-Romantic diagnosis of capitalist Masochism.

The Masochism of Capitalist Consumption

Given his aims, Weber's narrow focus on Luther and Calvinism in the sixteenth and seventeenth centuries was sensible and fruitful. But several other, very different, strains of Protestantism—including Pietism and Arminianism—emerged and developed in the eighteenth and nineteenth centuries that for my purposes are equally important (Campbell 1987). For these strains, it was the experience and expression of strong emotions rather than devotion to a calling that signaled the likelihood of salvation. Inward-looking self-scrutiny rather than outward-looking worldly action continued to be paramount, but its aim now was to recognize and heighten feelings rather than suppress them. Contemplating and lamenting one's own sinfulness was one source of strong feelings, but contemplating and commiserating with the misfortune of others played an increasingly important role, especially as secularized features of these strains contributed to the rise of Sentimentalism and Romanticism. Alongside church sermons and services, romance and Gothic novels became increasingly popular vehicles for displaying, eliciting, and indulging in strong feelings—especially since, as in the Kantian contingent sublime, readers' personal well-being was not at stake.

Particularly with the growth of secular Romanticism, a rich inner emotional life came to be seen not just as a sign of salvation, but also as an antidote to the combination of abstract, impersonal, utilitarian rationality and competitive, predatory behavior prevailing in emergent capitalist market society. Hobbes had in the seventeenth century already proposed a public or political solution to what he called "the war of all against all" characterizing competitive capitalist society (which he projected back onto a hypothetical "state of nature"): rational human beings would give up whatever benefits they might secure from exercising power individually and freely submit instead to a state authority (the "Leviathan") established via a "social contract" to guarantee collective security and individual rights by exercising sovereign power over everyone. By the end of the nineteenth century, partly in connection with the growth of anarchist movements, two problems with Hobbes's state solution had become readily apparent. For one, postulating a state of nature over which rational agents freely choose to enter into a social contract to safeguard their rights obscures the violence necessary for the establishment and exercise of state authority to begin with and for maintaining what Weber (1946) called the "monopoly of the legitimate use of physical force." Equally important, every new right won from and thereafter recognized by the state in fact increases its power over yet another aspect of personal and social life.[20] Writing as a historian in the wake of the defeat of the 1848 revolutions throughout Europe, and identifying strongly with various Eastern European minorities including not only his fellow Galicians but also Jews and Ruthenian peasants in their struggles within the Hapsburg Empire, Masoch was acutely aware of the failures of the Hobbesian state solution.[21] However, as atomistic market competition in the public sphere grew steadily more intense over the course of the nineteenth century, a very different, private solution to capitalist competition emerged: the domestic sphere as "haven in a heartless world." Writing as a novelist, it is this private sphere that Masoch examined in much of his fiction, of which the best known and clearest example is *Venus in Furs* (published in 1870).

The nineteenth century witnessed the emergence of a distinctly modern domestic space throughout Europe (at differing rates in different regions, to be sure), for both demographic and economic reasons. Demographic shifts favored cities, and in cities the place of work became increasingly separate from the place of residence, whereas in the countryside, they for the most part coincided. Meanwhile, as the market pervaded more and more areas of social life, production became increasingly distinct from consumption (especially, again, in cities), and the domestic sphere became the prime locus of consumption. As Carol Pateman (1988) has shown, the shift from a traditional society based on status and what she calls "paternal patriarchy" to a modern society based on contracts and fraternal patriarchy entailed not just the "social contract" itself and the myriad contracts negotiated in the public sphere, but a "sexual contract" governing the private sphere. And the overall effect of this modern sexual contract was to subordinate women by confining them to the domestic sphere and making them dependent on wage-earning men, who prevailed in the public sphere yet were free, unlike women, to operate in both.

But over the course of the nineteenth century, as social standing came to depend less on fixed and largely inherited status and more on wealth as demonstrated by conspicuous consumption, women's relegation to the domestic sphere took on a historically specific form: not just "trophy wives" themselves, married women were also charged with optimizing household consumption with displays of "good taste" so as to establish and continually improve their husbands' social standing—a charge facilitated by the rapid development at this time of shopping arcades, department stores, window shopping, advertising, and consumer credit (Williams 1982; Watson 1999; Lysack 2008). In this context, a man's home wasn't *his* castle, but *hers*: there, it was her taste that reigned supreme. Ironically enough, the domestic sphere as the locus of women's social subordination was simultaneously the locus of men's matrimonial subordination: as Benno, the masochist protagonist of Lou Andreas-Salomé's 1898 novella *Deviations* puts it, wives were "the women who rescue us from the wasteland of the soul, who provide the complement to the monotony of our professional existence" (Andreas-Salomé 1990, 75).[22] Ultimately, consumerism would become compensation in the private sphere for the loss of sovereignty in the public sphere for both sexes, whether that loss occurred through simple exclusion, for women, or through subservience to the vagaries of market competition and/or the boss, for men (Princen 2005, 65, 75–76).[23]

René Girard's (1965) study of the modern novel traces something akin to the evolution of patriarchal to fraternal patriarchy in terms of the changing position of what he calls the "mediators of desire." In the early modern novel, characters' desires are modeled on what Girard calls "transcendent mediators," whose plane of existence remains far superior to that of the characters themselves; Cervantes's *Don Quixote* provides a quintessential example—an elderly knight whose reading of romance novels leads to vain attempts to live up to an ideal of knighthood that ordinary mortals cannot possibly achieve. Gradually, the mediator descends from the ideal realm to occupy the same plane of existence as the characters; yet these immanent mediators are not just models of desire; they have also become rivals for the objects of desire, which anyone is in principle—and with sufficient income—perfectly capable of obtaining. So Girard characterizes this romantic, immanently mediated form of desire as "masochistic" (in the Freudian sense of self-defeating "moral masochism" rather than explicitly sexual masochism), inasmuch as the model of desire simultaneously represents a potential obstacle to obtaining the object of that desire. This is good as far as it goes—one of the ironies or paradoxes of mass consumption being that the very affordability of whatever product the consumer buys to establish their singular identity means that almost anyone else can buy it, too, thereby destroying the effect of singularity.[24] But this characterization is in crucial ways incomplete.

For what Girard surprisingly fails to observe is that this immanently mediated form of desire mirrors the form of market-mediated desire—and prevails in the novels he studies at precisely the same time that the capitalist market is transforming Western society in its own image (Goldmann 1975). What stands between and mediates the relation of desiring subjects to the objects of their desires is not merely models, but money, the marketplace, and marketing. Of course, desire may well have always been mediated by role models and images of various kinds. What is distinctive about nineteenth-century modernity is that the locus of these models increasingly coincides with the position of exchange value on the market, and the market—with its shopping arcades, department stores, mass-media advertising, and consumer credit—becomes the predominant platform for their circulation throughout society. This coincidence would prompt Mallarmé (2012) to declare that the cultural crisis of his time boiled down to the relation between "aesthetics and political economy." Fashion was, of course, the first and preeminent industry where models in mass circulation served to train consumer taste on given styles of apparel so as to simultaneously signal consumers' social standing and assure profitable returns on investment; fashion advertising and commentary were in fact mainstays of early commercial print culture. But the nineteenth century also witnessed an explosion of other consumer goods—what the French call "bibelots" (knickknacks)—that transformed the domestic interior, too, into a showplace for displaying the good taste and social standing of the household (Watson 1999). The domestic sphere became not just a haven in a heartless world, but the prime locus for translating purchasing power into a sense of personal identity and a claim on standing in society. The establishment of personal identity through advertising and domestic consumption led to the development of a style of pleasure-seeking specific to market society, which Colin Campbell (1987) has called "imaginative hedonism." In commercial culture, pleasure is found as much in imagining the purchase and use of advertised commodities as in actually owning and using them. And novels, along with mass-circulation newspapers and magazines, not only counted among the commodities purchased for use at home: they also furthered the development of imaginative hedonism by serving as vehicles for the circulation of models of consumption through their exhaustive descriptions of domestic décor, sartorial fashion, and leisure activities.

What remains suggestive in Girard's analysis is his identification of the vocation of the novels he examines: to diagnose not just what he calls the "masochism" of mass consumerism, but the failure of romantic desire to produce the desired result: a singular or authentic identity. Exposing the lie of romanticism, as the original French title has it, becomes the truth of the novel: *mensonge romantique e[s]t vérité romanesque*. And here the quintessential example is none other than Flaubert's Mme. Bovary, who grows up on romance novels, like Don Quixote before her; searches vainly for an ideal romantic love; and kills herself unable to repay the loans for the dresses and furnishings with which she tried to enhance the elegance and household standing of her boorish doctor-husband. Indeed, the basis for suspense in the plot structure of most Victorian novels typically revolves around the question of whether matrimonial borrowing and investments like the ones Emma makes in the Bovary household will pay off or not.[25] Masoch's novels, however, do more than expose the failures of romantic desire: they serve to diagnose capitalist consumerism as Masochistic. And this diagnostic vocation can be brought into sharper relief by returning to the contrast between Masochean and Sadean discourse.

Sade's hyperrational novels, as we have seen, alternate between reiterations of and justifications for endlessly repeated acts of torture; Masoch's novels, by contrast, are hypersensual: they are characterized by continuous and never-ending suspense, with action frozen to allow for long descriptions of static tableaux.[26] In psychodynamic terms, the rhythm of Sadean discourse repeats the release of tension through action, whereas Masochean discourse increases tension by repeatedly describing settings instead of narrating action. In a word, gratification in Sadism is endlessly repeated; gratification in Masochism is endlessly deferred. Perhaps the most important contrast is this: whereas the Sadean institution is governed by impersonal rules presented as eternal and universal, the Masochean scenario is governed by a contract drawn up between two intimates that applies only to the two of them and only for a specified period of time; and it takes place in the private sphere, in lavishly portrayed domestic interiors that had by Masoch's time become the prime site of consumerism.

Now in order for this domestic space to serve as an effective antidote to the ruthless competition prevailing on the capitalist market, the Masochean contract will have to achieve two related aims: eliminate any paternal or fraternal mediation between the subject and object of desire and extinguish all predatory behavior on the part of the desiring subject while nevertheless enabling him to obtain the object of his desire. And that is precisely what the terms of the Masochean contract accomplish. They call for an alliance between the subservient Masochist and an imperious woman, thereby creating a (domestic) space free from male power, paternal authority, and fraternal competition. In psychodynamic terms, where Sadists identify with the superego and project the ego onto the victims they punish, the Masochean scenario involves disavowing the superego and identifying with an idealized "ideal ego" stripped of power and any predatory designs on the woman. To the contrary, the contract endows her with all the power and enjoins her to dominate, humiliate, and torture the Masochist even though he has in fact done nothing to deserve such punishment.[27] And here is the payoff for the Masochist: voluntarily submitting to punishment that is completely undeserved ends up invalidating the punishment and thereby sanctioning intimate relations with the woman as object of desire that paternal authority or fraternal rivalry would ordinarily proscribe or prevent—even if such relations amount to little more than sitting quietly at her feet to bask in her company and luxuriate vicariously in the tasteful elegance of her furs and sumptuous interior decor. The ultimate aim of the Masochean contract is thus not simply to take pleasure in pain, but to endure undeserved punishment in order to invalidate it and to create an idealized private identity through the shared enjoyment of luxury in the domestic sphere.

The Masochean contract is key to the diagnostic vocation of Masoch's novels for a number of reasons. In contrast with Sade's novels, whose critical force derives as we have seen from their satirical use of bodily pain and abjection to challenge the ideals by which Sadistic torture is rationalized, the critical force of Masoch's novels arises from the ways they subject contract to parody and ultimately to narrative failure. In principle, contracts are supposed to operate to the mutual benefit of both parties. The Masochean contract, however, operates to the exclusive benefit of the imperious woman who wields power and to the apparent detriment of the Masochist, who suffers pain and humiliation. Historically, it is no accident that the contract would be the prime target of Masoch's parody. For one thing, contemporary anarchist movements suggested that despite its claims to benevolence, the social contract actually enhances the power of the state to the detriment of the well-being of its citizens. Similar claims were made regarding labor contracts, which became more widespread with the acceleration of capitalist production relations throughout Europe (and elsewhere) following the defeats of 1848 (Hobsbawm 1975). Entered into "willingly," the labor contract nevertheless consolidates and increases the power of capital over labor by guaranteeing and stabilizing the extraction of surplus value.[28] Most important, however, is the fact that the realization of surplus value through the sale of goods becomes during Masoch's lifetime just as important as the extraction of surplus value through capitalist production.

The importance of the realization of surplus value can be seen by returning to the distinction between the two primary forms of private property operative in capitalist society. There is property that is owned privately and used privately: consumer goods. And there is property that is owned privately but used collectively in production: capital goods. Specifically Masochean Masochism arises at the intersection of these two types of private property. Corresponding to these two types of private property are two distinct circuits of money in the capitalist economy, which are only tangentially related; they touch at only one point, and it is there that Masochism occurs.[29] One circuit contains the money paid out by the capitalist in the form of salaries as per the labor contract and then repaid to the capitalist in the purchase of consumer goods. This is the circuit of reproduction: the reproduction of labor power and of socialized subjects through consumption in the domestic sphere. Capitalist reproduction forms a closed circuit, in the sense that any increase in the size of the labor pool (under conditions of labor-market competition) decreases the cost of labor, and any intensification of socialization affixes purchasing power on the consumer goods produced and marketed by capital. The other circuit of money involves the production, reinvestment, and accumulation of capital on an ever-expanding scale; it takes the form of an ascending line or an ever-widening spiral, as funds are loaned by banks to productive enterprises and then repaid with interest. What is essential about these two circuits of money is that the first feeds the second: realizing surplus value by selling goods back to consumers at a profit makes an ever-greater amount of capital available to capitalists for reinvestment in further cycles of production and consumption. Every purchase made, whatever consumer-based private identity it may consolidate, contributes directly and inevitably to the realization of surplus value and to greater and greater capital accumulation. Even if the constitution of personal identity through consumption in the domestic sphere serves to compensate for the loss or degradation of identity at work or in the public sphere more generally, it nevertheless also continually increases the power of capital over both production and consumption and over society as a whole—and thus stands condemned as Masochistic in the properly Masochean sense of the term.

But the critical force of Masoch's fiction is not limited to parody. For not only is the contract central to the Masochean scenario subjected to parody, but it is also breached near the end of the story with the appearance of another man. Crucially, the Masochean scenario is embedded within a narrative where—just as at the end of *Madame Bovary*—reality reasserts its prerogatives and ends up annihilating the domestic ideal.[30] A prohibitory male authority figure returns to interrupt the idyllic scenario, the woman's allegiance shifts abruptly to the intruder, and she betrays the terms of the contract by joining with him in administering pain and humiliation on her terms rather than those of the contract. This is anathema to the Masochist, who derives no pleasure or satisfaction whatsoever from pain or punishments that lie outside the Masochean contract. This narrative conclusion is significant for at least two reasons. First of all, it shows that Masochean Masochism is not simply about taking pleasure in pain, but also about submitting to punishments intended to cleanse the Masochist of predatory designs on the woman in order to share in enjoying with her the luxuries of the domestic sphere safe from the oppression and humiliations of the public sphere. More important, it shows that the personal solution to the brutality of capitalist competition, based on establishing a compensatory idealized identity through private consumption, is not just Masochistic; it is ultimately untenable.

The conclusive narrative failure of the Masochean scenario is significant for one additional reason, which points beyond Masochism itself. For not only does Masoch's hero deeply resent the torture meted out by his erstwhile partner in realignment with paternal-fraternal authority: he is enraged by her betrayal and vows to take violent revenge on her and her male consort. He thus appears, read in light of subsequent developments, to be on the verge of what some twentieth-century psychologists have called "borderline conditions"—one term among many through which to examine the next stage in the evolution of capitalist culture.

Chapter Two

Borderline Conditions and Global Capitalism

In and of itself, Masochism proves to be a self-defeating strategy for negotiating the capitalist market, at least according to the diagnosis provided by Masoch's novels. That diagnosis is confirmed in a novel written nearly a century later by Georges Perec, when consumerism in France exploded due to the postwar economic boom known as "les trente glorieuses" (roughly 1945–75). Jerome and Sylvie, the main characters of Perec's *Les Choses* (1990; literally "Things") have succumbed so completely to consumerism that their lives revolve around window shopping and imagining all the wonderful "things" they could buy and do, if they only had enough money. Indeed, the entire first chapter of the novel is written in the conditional tense, describing room by room in meticulous detail how their apartment would be furnished, how their daily life would unfold, how "a whole life could be led harmoniously between [their] book-lined walls" (25). Utterly devoted to the pleasures of imaginative hedonism, they voluntarily choose to remain what we today call "gig workers," refusing to sacrifice their leisure time and flea-market shopping sprees to the deadening routines of regular employment or the prospects of career advancement. But gambling everything on the private solution of consumerism does not pay off: possessed by "a single passion, the passion for a higher standard of living" (35), inhabiting a consumer culture where it is a "social law . . . always to wish for more than you could have," they find themselves "forever one rung down on the ladder" (50), often spending what should have been their precious leisure time scrambling for the next gig, falling "only intermittently" into the "genuine debt" (45) to which Mme. Bovary succumbed, but never having enough money to buy all the things they so desperately crave. So eventually, tired of "think[ing] they are dying from things being too small, too cramped" (123), they resign themselves to the career track and set out by train in the last chapter (written entirely in the future tense) to run a branch advertising agency in Bordeaux. Executive salaries will enable them to afford many of the things they had only dreamed of before, and their elegant first-class accommodations will appear to promise them a "sumptuous feast" (126) in the dining car. "But the meal they will be served," Perec's narrator warns us, "will be downright tasteless" (126).

Imaginative hedonism can serve as the "spirit of modern consumerism" (Campbell 1987) in that the imagined anticipation of satisfaction so often exceeds whatever satisfaction may or may not be actually achieved, thereby continually fueling further consumption. The conclusion of Perec's novel—which is aptly subtitled *Une histoire des années soixantes* (A Story [or History] of the '60s) and is both set and written in the mid-1960s—may well be less cataclysmic than Masoch's, yet it too shows that consumerism is self-defeating on its own terms, even before the bill comes due. But in fact, of course, the bill does come due—as it did in this case when the first oil shock of 1973 put an abrupt end to the easy, Gilded Age consumerism of "les trente glorieuses." The oil crises of the 1970s and 1980s mark another historical turning point in the all-too-familiar boom-and-bust cycles that have characterized capitalist development for centuries, with prosperity giving way to austerity.

What distinguishes this turning point from earlier ones is the degree to which capitalism has by now become truly global in scope. The relations of production and the relations of consumption diagnosed by Sade and Masoch, respectively, are now literally worlds apart, both geographically and morally. Each of the capitalist perversions, as we have seen, provided a way of locking conflicting drives or components into a relatively stable, albeit unbalanced, configuration: Sadism entailed identifying with an inflated superego and projecting aspects of the ego onto others in order to punish them repeatedly, while Masochism entailed denying the authority of the superego for as long as possible in order to identify with a purified ideal ego. But with the expansion of capitalism to global scale, such relatively stable configurations no longer predominate, and psychic splitting becomes a predominant defense. As second-generation psychoanalysts could not help but observe, the neurotics and perverts central to Freud's theory and practice were in their time becoming rare; taking their place on the couch were patients with a plethora of disorders, generally characterized by psychic fragmentation, instability, and a weakening of the ego bordering on psychosis.[1] Indeed, the umbrella term *borderline conditions* locates these psychic configurations on an imagined border between neurosis and full-blown psychosis. Other terms, meanwhile, highlight various aspects of these configurations: in *dissociative identity disorder*, facets of the ego are split off and in extreme cases can even form discrete personalities (formerly known as "multiple personalities"); *schizophrenia* and *autism* refer to disturbances of weakened egos' capacity to synthesize experience, in both the short term (linking moments together in continuous experience) and the long term (recognizing objects from past experience).

Yet this shift from ego-strengthening to ego-weakening psychic configurations cannot be attributed to the widening gap between production and consumption alone: the expansion of the world market also fosters an increase in specialization, most obviously with the division of labor as production processes get more and more complex, but also with what we can call the division of leisure: the multiplication of niche consumer markets, increasingly differentiated lifestyles, commodity choices, and leisure-time pursuits.[2] Writing just a few years before Perec, sociologist Erving Goffman (1959) saw fit to analyze social interaction in terms of the various masks people wear in different situations. Increasing specialization effectively multiplies the number of different social roles individuals are called upon to perform: not just producer and consumer, but let's say architectural draughtsman, husband or wife, culinary foodie, soccer fan, father or mother, video gamer, country music aficionado, pool shark, amateur musician, gardener, and so on. This multiplication of disparate social roles makes it increasingly difficult and unlikely, if not impossible, that such a plethora of social roles could be integrated into a single self.

Indeed, one of the main disadvantages of Goffman's "dramaturgical" model and metaphors was the implication that there is an authentic self "behind the masks," a supposedly real actor behind the various and increasingly differentiated roles and scripts people are called upon to perform—an assumption that the Zimbardo prison experiment has since effectively debunked.[3] We also now know that the brain is continually rewiring and reprogramming itself in response to different situations and that belief in a stable self behind the masks depends largely on the stories we are able to tell ourselves and others about our selves. Psychic continuity and coherence are now understood to be products of narrative continuity and coherence. And ironically enough, literary narrative—in its modernist and postmodernist forms, at least, with the *Nouveau Roman* as perhaps the clearest example—has contributed as much to this diagnosis as psychology and philosophy, precisely by staging the breakdown of temporal continuity and narrative coherence.

Decades before the emergence of the *Nouveau Roman*, Sartre's *Nausea* (1964) challenged the notion that human existence is susceptible to narrativization. The novel's main character, Antoine Roquentin, has moved to a provincial French town to research and write the biography of a late-eighteenth-century nobleman, the Marquis de Rollebon, but abandons the project as he discovers that capturing the life of someone long dead in narrative form is impossible. He realizes that he is imposing order on facts that have no order of their own: "[I formulate] honest hypotheses which take the facts into account: but I sense so definitely that they come from me, and that they are simply a way of unifying my own knowledge. Not a glimmer comes from Rollebon's side. Slow, lazy, sulky, the facts adapt themselves to the rigour of the order I wish to give them; but it remains outside of them" (23).

But as soon as he abandons Rollebon, Roquentin realizes that the biographical project was the only unifying thread giving his own life meaning: "I no longer existed in myself, but in him; I ate for him, breathed for him, each of my movements had its sense outside . . . of me, in him" (133). So now it is no longer just Rollebon's life that lacks or indeed defies narrative coherence, but his own as well. The past, both his and Rollebon's, has ceased to exist (132, 209); all that exists are isolated present moments "without a past, without a future" (235). Henceforth, Roquentin concludes, there is nothing he can do but "outlive [him]self" (210). This loss of temporal continuity and the reduction of time to isolated present moments is one of the distinctive features of schizophrenia as defined by Jacques Lacan and mobilized by Fredric Jameson, among others, to diagnose the twentieth-century breakdown of narrative (Jameson 1991; Heise 1997; Lyotard 1984).

Yet Roquentin's discovery that Rollebon's life and his own are not susceptible to narrativization takes place, ironically enough, within another narrative of discovery designed to explain the bouts of nausea from which the novel gets its name. For the novel consists almost entirely (aside from a brief editors' note at the beginning) of the diary kept by Roquentin to trace the sequence of increasingly disturbing experiences that gradually lead him to the conclusion that human existence is absurd. Indeed, once Roquentin has abandoned his biographical project, it is the nausea narrative that provides the only unifying thread to give his life meaning. But it is a thread that unravels itself: having learned that human existence is incompatible with narrative form, Roquentin ends his diary planning to write fiction instead of historical biography. For unlike biography, fiction does not impose narrative form on human existence, but stands on its own—much like the musical melody ("Some of these Days") that so fascinates him.

For our purposes, more important than the self-deconstructing narrative that concludes by rejecting narrative form and declaring human existence to be absurd is the nature of the nausea that leads Roquentin to this conclusion. His intensifying bouts of nausea culminate in a confrontation with a chestnut-tree root in a city park. "Suddenly," he says, "the veil is torn away, I have understood, I have seen. [. . .] [M]y goal is reached: I know what I wanted to know; I have understood all that has happened to me since January" (170). Faced with the chestnut-tree root, he "couldn't remember it was a root any more. The words had vanished and with them the significance of things" (170–71). Try as he might, at the height of nausea, Roquentin can no longer recognize the things around him, and it is this failure of recognition that leaves him face to face with bare existence, with a meaningless world out of which he can no longer make any sense. Looking back on this culminating experience of meaningless existence, he will adopt the term *absurdity* as the "key to Existence, the key to [his] Nauseas, the key to [his] own life" (173), thereby converting what might be considered a cognitive disorder into the key discovery of existentialism. Alongside the loss of temporal continuity, this failure of recognition is another distinctive feature of schizophrenia.[4] In more conventional psychological terms, the schizophrenia diagnosed by Sartre in *Nausea* involves the breakdown of both short-term and long-term memory: both the ability to synthesize a present moment into an on-going temporal unity in the short term, and the ability to subsume a present perception under a category developed over the long term.

Sartre's novel charts the discovery of the kind of absurdity that Meursault, the antihero of Camus's *The Stranger* (1989), is already living. And where Roquentin's trajectory leads him to experiences resembling schizophrenia, the experience of Camus's character manifests traits more readily associated with autism. Among the most salient is difficulty filtering sensations, which often leads to being overwhelmed by them (Chien et al. 2019; Crasta et al. 2021). Nowhere is this more in evidence than in the novel's climactic scene in which Meursault shoots the Arab on the beach; given the dramatic conclusion to the episode, it is easy to overlook how extensive the references to being overwhelmed by sensations actually are:

> We walked on the beach for a long time. By now the sun was over-powering. It shattered into little pieces on the sand and water. (55)
>
> With every blade of light that flashed off the sand, from a bleached shell or a piece of broken glass, my jaws tightened. (57)
>
> Most of the time, [the Arab] was just a form shimmering before my eyes in the fiery air . . . . It was the same sun, the same light still shining on the same sand as before. (58)
>
> Without getting up, the Arab drew his knife and held it up to me in the sun. The light shot off the steel and it was like a long flashing blade cutting at my forehead. [. . .] All I could feel were the cymbals of sunlight crashing on my forehead and, indistinctly, the dazzling spear flying up from the knife in front of me. The scorching blade slashed at my eyelashes and stabbed at my stinging eyes. That's when everything began to reel. [. . .] It seemed to me as if the sky split open from one end to the other to rain down fire. My whole being tensed and I squeezed my hand around the revolver. The trigger gave; I felt the smooth underside of the butt; and there, in that noise, sharp and deafening at the same time, is where it all started. (59)

In fact, references to being overwhelmed by sensations are found throughout the novel, both before and after the shooting:

> All of it—the sun, the smell of leather and horse dung from the hearse, the smell of varnish and incense, and my fatigue after a night without sleep—was making it hard for me to see or think straight. (17)
>
> [The Magistrate] went on . . . talking about my crime [for] so long . . . that finally all I was aware of was how hot a morning it was. (101)
>
> While my lawyer went on talking . . . I was assailed by memories of a life that wasn't mine anymore, but one in which I'd found the simplest and most lasting joys: the smells of summer, the part of town I loved, a certain evening sky, Marie's dresses and the way she laughed. (104)

Meursault's immersion in sensations produces and/or accompanies a chronic inability to understand and respond appropriately to what social situations and other people expect of him—another trait commonly associated with autism. In the quotation above, for example, his relationship with his girlfriend, Marie, is reduced to the dresses she wears and the way she laughs. When asked if he loved her, "[he] told her it didn't mean anything but that [he] didn't think so" (35); and when asked "if I wanted to marry her. I said it didn't make any difference to me and that we could if she wanted to" (41). He similarly defies expectations when his boss offers him a promotion and the chance to move to Paris and travel extensively: "I said yes but that really it was all the same to me. Then he asked me if I wasn't interested in a change of life. I said that people never change their lives, that in any case one life was as good as another and that I wasn't dissatisfied with mine here at all. He looked upset" (41). And in the end, Meursault's conviction hinges to a large extent on his inability to meet expectations of sadness at his mother's funeral and remorse for shooting the Arab:

> [His lawyer] asked if I had felt any sadness that day. The question caught me by surprise and . . . I answered that. . . . I probably did love Maman, but that didn't mean anything. . . . Here the lawyer interrupted me and he seemed very upset. He made me promise I wouldn't say that at my hearing or in front of the examining magistrate. I explained to him, however, that my nature was such that my physical needs often got in the way of my feelings. The day I buried Maman, I was very tired and sleepy, so much so that I wasn't really aware of what was going on. (65)
>
> I couldn't help admitting that [the prosecutor] was right. I didn't feel much remorse for what I'd done. But I . . . would have liked to have tried explaining to him . . . that I had never been able to truly feel remorse for anything. (100)

Meursault's failure to manifest the emotions expected of him in these dramatic social situations appears to others as signs of a shocking moral indifference.

A lesser-known feature of autism than difficulty managing sensations and others' expectations is delay in processing sense experience (Manning 2016). In this respect, autism resembles schizophrenia, except that while the latter entails a complete failure to subsume sense impressions under recognizable categories, autism involves merely a delay in doing so. Here, too, examples in the novel abound. In some cases, the delay seems linked to Meursault's difficulty processing sensations:

> I noticed that for quite some time the countryside had been buzzing with the sound of insects and the crackling of grass. (16)
>
> For the first time in months, I distinctly heard the sound of my own voice. I recognized it as the same one that had been ringing in my ears for many long days, and I realized that all that time I had been talking to myself. (81)

In other cases, it is his recognition of the expected aspects of a social situation such as his trial that is delayed:

> Then . . . I noticed a row of faces in front of me. They were all looking at me: I realized that they were the jury. (83)
>
> At first I hadn't realized that all those people were crowding [into the courtroom] to see me. . . . It took some doing on my part to understand that I was the cause of all the excitement. (83)
>
> After a five-minute recess . . . we heard the testimony of Celeste, who was called by the defense. "The defense" meant me. (91–02)
>
> [The prosecutor] reminded the court of my insensitivity; of my ignorance when asked Maman's age; of my swim the next day–with a woman . . . and finally of my taking Marie home with me. It took me a few minutes to understand the last part because he kept saying "his mistress" and to me she was Marie. (99)

Along with the difficulties managing sensations and others' expectations, Meursault's delayed processing of experience links his character to autism in much the same way as the breakdown of short- and long-term memory links Roquentin's character to schizophrenia.

It is worth repeating at this point that I am not aiming to diagnose these fictional characters (much less their authors) as clinically autistic or schizophrenic. For one thing, while both these categories were once thought to designate discrete entities, each is now understood to reference a spectrum, instead. It is no longer a matter of classifying someone as autistic or not, but of locating a range of more or less severe traits on the autism spectrum; similarly, behavior patterns of what was once considered "the" schizophrenic are now located on the schizophrenia spectrum. Indeed, if we single out the trait of difficulty with cognitive processing, the delay in recognizing objects of experience characteristic of autism appears as a less severe form of the inability or refusal to subsume objects under familiar categories characteristic of schizophrenia. The umbrella term *borderline conditions* (distinct from and broader than borderline personality disorder) has the advantage of referring to a general weakening or disintegration of the ego as evidenced by a range of traits, including some that are often also associated with autism and/or schizophrenia. Most important, though, is that the immense popularity and universally recognized cultural significance of these existentialist (anti)heroes justify using them to diagnose the sociohistorical conditions under which they achieved such widespread currency and acclaim.

Yet there are two difficulties in using these great existentialist novels alone for cultural diagnosis. For one thing, they are both written as first-person narratives. And as Lukács (1971b) was among the first of many to complain, the turn to first-person narration and even stream-of-consciousness made the modernist novel singularly ill equipped to diagnose the social determinants of the kinds of intimate but limited personal experience it expresses so well. And this generic shortcoming is only compounded when the novels in question conclude that life itself is meaningless or absurd. Yet as Walter Benjamin (1969, 158) said of Proust's great modernist novel, "Man's inner concerns do not have their issueless private character by nature." So for a diagnosis of the conditions portrayed in the existentialist novels, I will turn to the other end of the narrative spectrum and examine a commercial film whose main character has practically no inner life whatsoever. Unlike the novels just examined, Norman Jewison's *Rollerball* (1975) is a dystopia, a genre that maps society as a whole by distilling certain features of contemporary society which it then exaggerates and projects into the future. The film can thus be read as an allegory or x-ray analysis of contemporary social life, and it complements the novels by situating existentialism's central tenet, the meaningless of human existence, in an explicitly social and historical, rather than a universal or metaphysical, frame of reference.

Nominally, as the title suggests, it is the sport of roller derby that is thus exaggerated and projected onto an imaginary future society. The sport of rollerball is even more violent than roller derby, involving motorcycles, spike-studded gloves and helmets, and assorted other weapons; severe injury and even accidental death are regular and indeed thirsted-after aspects of the game. Like the novels in this respect, the story revolves around a single character, a rollerball superstar named Jonathan, and highlights his relations with the nameless transnational corporate elite that owns him and his team and that completely controls the whole society. The problem Jonathan faces is that, after his rise to superstardom through ruthless competition on the rollerball track, the corporate elite insists that he retire immediately from the game. For the function of rollerball, as the corporate director explains when Jonathan questions his retirement, is to demonstrate the futility of individual effort and the necessity of submitting to group rule—and Jonathan's stardom clearly betrays that principle. When he then claims the right to make his own decisions, Jonathan is told that on the contrary his role it to obey and that the corporate elite alone has the power to make decisions for the good of everyone. Yet Jonathan still refuses to retire—and so the corporation changes the rules of the game—no penalties, no substitutions—so that Jonathan will be deliberately killed by the opposing team in the next game. Like Meursault's in this respect, Jonathan's life is meaningless partly because he is enjoined to obey an irrational, imposed authority—but it is meaningless also because he is stripped of the freedom he craves to make his own decisions. The life he leads, just like the game he plays, is governed by rules he cannot alter and that are subject to change at any time by those in control.

Though governed by inflexible, irrational, and ultimately near-fatal rules on the job, Jonathan nonetheless enjoys considerable "freedom of choice" at home, where his superstar salary buys him all possible creature-comforts and luxury, including an endless series of ravishing "playmates" provided by the corporation. But here again, the only really meaningful choice—the woman he loves—has been ruled out by the corporation, who took her and reassigned her to an elite executive. No amount of substitute gratifications, as Freud would say, can satisfy his longing for the true object of his desire.

Faced with meaninglessness at work as well as at home, in his private as well as his professional life, Jonathan is driven to find out how the corporations came to power and what their grand design for society actually amounts to. His search leads him to a gigantic computer that runs this entirely administered society, and there he learns that the corporations took over after nationalism and international strife had almost destroyed the planet. But when Jonathan asks for what end the corporate elite now governs society peaceably, the computer is unable to reply: it becomes clear that social life is administered merely to perpetuate the existing capitalist power structure, with no prospect for improvement or change.

What *Rollerball* suggests, then, is that the meaninglessness of individual life is not some general metaphysical postulate but rather derives from the meaninglessness of social life itself, in a society proceeding on automatic pilot, as it were, with no aim except to preserve a class structure favoring the corporate-technocratic elite and the endless accumulation of capital. As a recognizable allegory (albeit a simplified and exaggerated one, as allegories usually are) of prevailing trends in contemporary society, the film is of particular significance: like the novels of Sade and Masoch, it can help turn an additional psychiatric category inside out to diagnose society rather than just individuals.

The psychiatric category at issue in the film is so-called borderline conditions (Kernberg 1975). The category is a controversial one, but it refers generally to a weakening of the ego's ability to negotiate relations among libidinal drives, social expectations, and reality—analyzed by Freud in terms of the pleasure principle (id), the superego, and the reality principle. Part of the controversy arises from the term itself, which is misleading if taken to imply a clear-cut dividing line between neurosis and psychosis. Instead, the term designates a spectrum of traits and behaviors that are neither neurotic nor psychotic but lie somewhere between the two, or better, combine features of each. Borderline conditions thus include a degree of impairment of reality testing, but not the absolute and lasting break with reality and the prevalence of delusions and hallucinations characteristic of full-blown psychosis. Roquentin's bouts of nausea, especially as epitomized in his encounter with the chestnut-tree root in the park, display this kind of trouble with reality testing. Borderline conditions can also involve a degree of difficulty anticipating, understanding, and/or responding appropriately to social expectations, but without the delusional paranoia or complete foreclosure of superego functions typical of psychosis. Here, Meursault provides an apt illustration. And last, borderline conditions involve a degree of difficulty mastering and integrating diverse drive impulses into a stable ego formation, with neither the rigidity of neurosis and perversion nor the radical incoherence and impulsiveness of psychosis. For this reason, borderline conditions are often closer to perversion than to neurosis in that drive impulses express themselves in desublimated form, unlike the sublimated forms of substitute gratification found in neuroses.

There is also considerable disagreement among practicing and theoretical psychiatrists as to whether borderline conditions are better defined by splitting or fragmentation. For Otto Kernberg (1975), following Melanie Klein, borderline conditions entail an inability to synthesize good and bad aspects of objects into a nuanced whole and a corresponding inability to tolerate ambiguity. Instead, borderline patients experience an all-or-nothing split between good objects and bad objects. But for Sander Abend, writing for the Kris Study Group (Abend 1983), borderline conditions entail an inability to synthesize a wide variety of drives and are therefore not as closely tied to unresolved conflicts between aggression and attraction. While these disagreements may have implications for divergent treatment strategies, there is widespread agreement that borderline conditions arise from strong fears of abandonment and ensuing feelings of insecurity. For our purposes, borderline conditions will be understood to encompass a range of psychic structures where either splitting or fragmentation or both result in egos whose ability to integrate reality testing, social expectations, and libidinal impulses is weaker than those of neurotics and perverts but stronger than those of psychotics.

Given the purpose of diagnosing and treating individuals, the psychiatric literature on borderline conditions rarely goes beyond family circumstances to explain their increasing prevalence over the last century or so, especially relative to the classical neuroses. However, this narrow focus on individual therapy risks masking important social determinations of borderline conditions—determinations that the psychoanalytic concept of *Nachträglichkeit* can help us recover. It is unnecessary to claim that family circumstances play no role whatsoever in borderline etiology. For however much or little inconsistent or conflicted parenting may have contributed during childhood to an inability to synthesize good and bad object representations, the ever-expanding capitalist market itself drives good and bad farther and farther apart, inasmuch as leisure and consumption are coded as good (and associated with personal freedom of choice and expression), while work is coded as bad (something you have to be paid to endure), and there is less and less of an intrinsic relation between the two. As for psychic fragmentation, increasing specialization in the spheres of leisure and consumption, as well as work, multiplies social roles and diversifies activities and modes of coping and gratification, making it more and more difficult for the ego to integrate them into a stable whole. And regardless of whether strong feelings of insecurity developed from absent or distant parenting during childhood, such feelings can always emerge in adulthood when the vagaries of the capitalist market threaten to dispossess anyone of their means of life at any moment and can also reinforce or exacerbate whatever feelings of insecurity may have obtained in childhood. The effect of dispossession in borderline conditions, however, is quite unlike the strengthening of the repetition compulsion found in Sadism and Masochism, for here the weakened ego's lack of impulse control and inconsistency of object choice mean that there is practically nothing for the repetition compulsion to repeat.

As useful as the broad concept of borderline conditions may be for registering some of the effects of the capitalist market on psychic structure and dynamics, there are a number of ways of responding to those conditions, three of which are outlined in what follows. One response is to try to shore up the ego despite its weaknesses. A second response resembles neurotic defenses that subordinate desire to social acceptability (sacrificing the id to superego prohibitions), while the third resembles perversions that subordinate social acceptability to drive gratification (sacrificing superego prohibitions to the id).

Borderline Narcissism

Perhaps the most obvious response to borderline conditions is to overcompensate for their ego weakening effects by fabricating a narcissistic "grandiose self." Borderline narcissism would thus constitute a defense mechanism or reaction formation to the absurd or meaningless conditions of social life and the corresponding disintegration of the individual psyche, even though the grandiose self remains very unstable. Like autism and schizophrenia, narcissistic personalities occupy a spectrum with varying degrees of severity. By analyzing narcissistic personalities in relation to the broader category of borderline conditions, Kernberg is able to distinguish three levels of borderline narcissism, each level manifesting more pronounced ego disintegration than the last.[5] The level of least disturbance describes the smoothly functioning, well-adapted narcissist, who often escapes diagnosis as such. The next level is narcissistic personality disorder, which almost always entails an underlying borderline condition. The third level is overt borderline narcissism, which sometimes includes outright antisocial traits as well (and of which Dostoevski's Underground Man might serve as a pertinent illustration).

The responses of our existentialist (anti)heroes to their borderline conditions clearly belong somewhere on this spectrum, probably on the end involving lesser degrees of disturbance. For who is unable to form lasting commitments to other people and institutions, if not Roquentin? He may get excited about his fits of nausea, but in relations with other people, he is as affectless, as unemotional as his counterpart, Meursault, is at the funeral of his mother or when he shoots the Arab on the beach. In fact, psychiatrists have taken Sartre's novel (and his early philosophy) as an apt illustration of this personality type (Klas and Offenkranz 1976). They note in Roquentin certain defensive patterns of response to the disintegration of self and experience that recur frequently in cases of narcissism: a kind of hyperreflective attention paid to the disintegrating self, as evidenced in

Roquentin's obsessive journal keeping; an attraction to music and especially to melody (e.g., "Some of these Days"), for the sense of temporal continuity it affords an ego whose own ability to synthesize is weak; and finally, two ways of relating to other people, which correspond to the basic forms of narcissistic transference observed in therapy. Roquentin first attempts a form of "idealizing transference" in relation to the subject of his biography, Rollebon, whose imposing figure confers value on his own existence (Sartre 1964, 98). But when he realizes that Rollebon is flawed (just like everyone else), he rejects both the historical personage and the biographical project in a typically narcissistic reversal. Roquentin then takes up a position (akin to narcissistic "mirror transference") of aloof disdain for other people, tinged with a mute and somewhat disparaging pity. Even events of some magnitude—such as the expulsion of the Self-made Man from the library (166–68) or the scene with the flasher in the park (79)—are gripping without being engaging: Roquentin remains frozen in his role of observer. This defensive aloofness—and the borderline personality splitting it implies—is perhaps most dramatically illustrated when Roquentin stabs himself in the arm—and then watches dispassionately as his blood trickles across the table (100). The point of highlighting the narcissism of Roquentin and Meursault is not to diagnose the characters or their authors, of course, but to diagnose the cultural milieu in which their importance as existentialist (anti)heroes achieved such widespread recognition.

To this end, the psychiatric literature can get us only so far. It cites three main factors in the etiology of borderline narcissism, all of which, unsurprisingly, are centered in the nuclear family:

1. First of all, a steady decline in paternal authority in the home, such that Oedipal struggle is never fully engaged, superego development is stunted, and the narcissist never fully gains control of s/his impulses and behaviors;

2. second, a growing ambivalence in maternal instinct, such that the child is alternately smothered with affection and denied affection altogether, either lavishly overstimulated or else denied any gratification whatsoever, and the narcissist's only response to deprivation and adversity is helpless rage;

3. finally, due to such parental inconsistency, good and bad, security and terror become absolutes, and the child is unable to develop a synthetic and complex, nuanced view of the

world, so the narcissist is plagued with exaggerated expectations—both positive and negative—of himself, other people, and society in general.

Without invalidating these familial factors, *Rollerball* proposes a different and additional etiology for borderline narcissism. For it shows that it is not just paternal authority that proves groundless and turns authoritarian, but social authority itself, vested in the corporate technocracy, which proves able to maintain absolute power over the masses by providing commodities and spectacles, but requires totally alienating work conditions and turns out to be thoroughly irrational in its long-term goals. And again, it is not just maternal instinct that turns ambivalent and induces continual frustration, but the very structure and dynamic of consumer society itself, which promises everyone instant and total satisfaction, yet can allow no one enough satisfaction—to stop consuming. Finally, it is not just parental inconsistencies that fragment the psyche and undermine the ego's synthesizing functions, but rather the radical split under capitalism between meaningless, exploited, alienated work and equally meaningless, commodified, administered leisure; between brutal competition on the job market—figured in the no-holds-barred violence of the rollerball star—and endless frustration on the commodity market—figured in his tragic romance; between, that is to say, the spheres of production and consumption in capitalist society. What such an allegorical reading of *Rollerball* against the backdrop of the existentialist tradition suggests, then, is that the source of widespread borderline narcissism is not primarily—or not only—the vicissitudes of modern family life, but rather the basic structure of capitalist social relations themselves.

There may appear to be residues of Sadism and Masochism in Jonathan's character: in the extreme desublimated violence he inflicts on other rollerball players and in the equally desublimated gratification of his playboy consumerism. But two important differences obtain. First of all, the residues of the two perversions converge here in a single character, whereas Sadism and Masochism proper each comprised a universe of its own. More importantly, Jonathan's borderline-narcissistic sadism is stripped of its relation to a superior abstract rationality and serves merely to assert his own superiority as a hypercompetitive rollerball superstar; he is an employee, not a capitalist. Similarly, his borderline-narcissistic masochism is stripped of any idealization of and subservience to an idolized woman and serves only to fuel his consumer hedonism; he treats his playmates as mere playthings for his personal enjoyment. Whereas each of the perversions consolidates an ego fixated on a specific regime of torture and suffering, borderline narcissists oscillate between the two in a desperate, and in Jonathan's case a failed, attempt to endow their life with meaning.

A similar diagnosis is available in a novel published little more than a decade after *Rollerball*: Brett Ellis's *American Psycho* (1991).[6] If Roquentin and Meursault can be located at the nearly normal, adaptive end of the borderline-narcissistic spectrum, Ellis's Patrick Bateman clearly occupies the other, nearly psychotic, antisocial end, combining the vapid consumerism of Jerome and Sylvie with the ruthless and nearly lethal violence of Jonathan. As the title clearly indicates, this novel is a followup to Hitchcock's famous horror movie, *Psycho*. Hitchcock had revolutionized the horror film genre by shifting its setting from gothic castles in far-off lands to the motel next door. Ellis shifts the setting once again, focusing squarely on the capitalist elite of Wall Street, with their posh penthouse condos, summer places in the Hamptons, and the exclusive restaurants and fitness clubs they frequent. The novel's story line, such as it is, involves an endless series of vapid vignettes of Bateman having meals or drinks with his friends, catalogue-like descriptions of what they are wearing, eating, and/or drinking, the home furnishings and entertainment equipment they own—all laced with increasingly gruesome depictions of the torture he inflicts and the murders he commits. Significantly, we never actually see Bateman working (although we do learn the designer-names of his office furniture): rather, he—along with all his friends—are depicted as quintessential consumers. Indeed, while the narrative carefully identifies the brand name of the clothes worn by all the characters, their actual names and identities are often confused or unclear: people have become so interchangeable that the only thing that stands out is the commodities they purchase, the restaurants they go to, and so on. One part of the meager plot in fact turns on the fact that the rival stockbroker Bateman kills is so often mistaken for other people in their circle that no one is sure whether he is missing or not.

The story revolves, then, around coldblooded competition and egocentric consumerism. Bateman is obsessed with having the best designer clothes, the best salon tan, the best table at the best restaurants, the best stereo, and so on and so on. At the same time, he is obsessed with business competition: he gets insanely envious when one rival appears to have a more elegant business card than he does, or when he learns another rival has an expensive tanning bed in his own home; he kills another competitor who handles a bigger account than he does; after a conversation about how the Japanese economy is outperforming the American economy, he kills a poor

Asian delivery boy—only to find out he's Chinese rather than Japanese. Much of Bateman's irrepressible rage indeed results directly from this maniacal competitiveness—although he also kills a number of helpless bums he loathes precisely because of their vulnerability and their inability to compete.

Much of his murderous rage, especially later in the novel, is directed against women, who are also often associated with vulnerability or with the capacity to make men feel vulnerable. To Bateman, women represent the threat of intimacy, mutual consideration, and emotional attachment—aspects of human being that are anathema to his competitive spirit. The extremity of the sexually degrading and ultimately murderous violence he exercises against them is presented as a desperate defense against traits such as love, intimacy, and commitment that would risk interfering with his ability to compete. Bateman has become not just interchangeable with the other Wall Street capitalists, as he himself admits, but almost completely inhuman: he is not much of a character—more a hyperbolic personification of ruthless capitalist competition and consumerism gone amok. And like Jonathan's, his violence and greed are devoid of any relation to loftier ideals of the kind obtaining for Sadism and Masochism proper: they are strictly self-serving, egocentric—and thus make for a fitting diagnosis of borderline narcissism.

Borderline Supremacists

While borderline narcissists try to shore up the weakened ego, borderline supremacists identify instead with the superego. The term *borderline supremacist*, especially in the plural, is more useful than other, more familiar near synonyms such as *fascist* or *authoritarian personality* for a number of reasons. For one thing, it underscores the ego weakness of supremacists, particularly as regards realty testing, consistency, and impulse control: supremacists are notoriously prone to conspiracy theories; they are largely immune to argument because they so successfully compartmentalize issues that they don't recognize self-contradiction or hypocrisy; they tend to lash out at those who disagree or differ from them in some way. More significantly, supremacism takes a number of different forms: best known, and perhaps most important, is white supremacism, also known as racism; but there are also Aryan supremacists (a.k.a. Nazis and neo-Nazis), heterosupremacists (a.k.a. homophobes), male supremacists (misogynists), Christian supremacists (Christian nationalists, many "born-again" evangelicals and some anti-Semites), American supremacists ("exceptionalists" or national chauvinists), and many others.

The point of subsuming these varied manifestations under one category is to highlight the psychic structure and psychodynamics they share: the tendency to overcompensate for ego weakness not by concentrating on the ego itself, but by identifying with the superego—often, though not always, as incarnated in a prominent and powerful authority figure.

In Richard Wright's *Native Son* (1940), Bigger Thomas's lawyer, Max, identifies the kernel of this syndrome in terms of what he calls the "guilt-fear" complex expressed by the enraged white mob howling outside the courtroom for Bigger's execution. "There is guilt in the rage that demands that this man's life be snuffed out so quickly!" Max declares, "Fear and hate and guilt are the keynotes of this drama!" (300). And his point is that it is not just Bigger, but the white mob, too, that feels guilt: "Deep down in them they feel like you, Bigger" (326). "Guilt-fear is the basic tone of the prosecution and of the people in this case. In their hearts they feel that a wrong has been done and when a Negro commits a crime against them, they fancy they see the ghastly evidence of that wrong" (302). The guilt is shared because "on both sides men . . . are fighting for life" (326), and while Bigger has destroyed two lives, white supremacism has destroyed untold thousands, including Bigger's own: "Each of them—the mob and the mob-masters; the wire-pullers and the frightened; the leaders and their pet vassals—know and feel that their lives are built upon a historical deed of wrong against many people. . . . Their feeling of guilt is as deep as that of the boy who sits here on trial" (300). This shared guilt is the basis of the white mob's unconscious identification with Bigger, which nevertheless fuels their rage and thirst for wreaking vengeance upon him. For this is a peculiar form of identification, which can be called *punitive projective identification*. Unconscious identification with an apparently guilty party enables the white supremacists to split off and project their own guilt onto an external other and punish it there; the ego disavows responsibility for its own actions and sides with the punitive superego against the split-off part of the ego.

A quarter of a century after Wright, Richard Hofstadter included projective identification in a set of traits of the "paranoid style" in politics he found throughout American history: he declared it "hard to resist the conclusion that [the supremacists'] enemy is on many counts a projection of the self," for "exponents of the paranoid style . . . [tend] to project and express unacknowledgeable aspects of their own psychological concerns" (1965, 85). And the paranoid style in American politics is not limited to white Americans' guilt-fear of African Americans: among its other targets dating back to the late eighteenth-century, Hofstadter lists Illuminists,

Masons, Jesuits, and more recently, Communists. Nor is punitive projective identification the only trait shared by exponents of the paranoid style: they tend to see the world in terms of a split between absolute good and absolute evil that is too irremediable for politics to handle; and because of the vast conspiracy they see arrayed against themselves, they see little hope of averting apocalypse through ordinary measures.

Punitive projective identification is also central to what is probably the most famous analysis of supremacism, Theodor Adorno and colleagues' (1950) postwar study of what they called "the authoritarian personality."[7] Although it combines several of the nine traits identified by Adorno and colleagues as comprising the authoritarian personality, Adorno claimed that the combination of submissiveness to established authority and aggressiveness directed against perceived inferiors was the "main characteristic" of what he sometimes called the "fascist character" (often in quotation marks).[8] A more complete sketch of the authoritarian personality emerges from combining all nine traits (listed in parentheses): Identification with a punitive superego is evident in supremacists' uncritical subscription to the conventional values of idealized moral authority ("conventionalism" and "authoritarian submission") and their affinity for toughness, dominance, and the exercise of power ("power"). Thinking in rigid categories ("stereotypy"), especially involving the us-versus-them categorization favored by Nazi theorist Carl Schmitt, combines with a generalized hostility ("cynicism") and a tendency to project unconscious impulses outward ("projectivity") to seek punishment ("authoritarian aggression") for those who do not subscribe to conventional values, those who are perceived as weak, imaginative, or "tender-minded" ("anti-intraception"), and/or those who are openly sexual ("sex").

As Adorno was the first to admit, recourse to psychoanalysis in an empirical study based on questionnaires and interviews was both a strength and a weakness: it enabled the research team to identify in the authoritarian personality a propensity for fascism where overt fascist behavior was not present; but it also foregrounded individual and family circumstances instead of the "social forces" he insisted were ultimately responsible for such a propensity.[9] But the "authoritarian personality" is best understood not as a fixed character structure determined by child rearing, but as a set of attitudes, behaviors, and defense mechanisms developed in response to specific social forces. I have already identified some of those social forces: desublimation of aggressivity from competition on the job market, especially under neoliberalism, and desublimation of cupidity from consumer hedonism to prevent crises of overproduction both decrease the ego's drive-management capacity. The stimulation of consumer hedonism through the implementation of retail credit not only addresses capital's chronic crises of overproduction, but breeds subjects wracked by guilt (*Schuld*) about the debts (*Schulden*) they owe and by fears about paying them off. The subordination of use value and meaning to exchange value weakens the ego's reality-testing abilities, and the multiplication of specialized roles due to the increased divisions of labor and leisure combined with the fragmentation of social authority due to the formal rationality of burgeoning disparate bureaucracies weaken its ability to synthesize. Fragmentation of the ego is then exacerbated by splitting due to the growing gap between production and consumption. But another way to bring to the fore the social forces behind borderline supremacism is to examine and compare a variety of historical instances.

I will start with Aryan supremacism, which has been the subject of much research, of which the most relevant for our purposes is Klaus Theweleit's (1987) study of the fantasy life of Freikorps paramilitary groups, composed largely of World War I veterans in pre-Nazi Germany. At the core of the "male fantasies" of Freikorps soldiers lies a drastic imbalance between the self-conceptions of the male soldiers and their split image of women, and particularly of female sexuality. In Freikorps fantasies (and often enough in their actions), an a-sexual "white" woman was idealized and offered protection; a sexual "red" woman was feared, demonized, and slaughtered. The red woman represents pleasure and sharing, in all of their many forms and combinations, from sensuous joy and fusion with others to prostitution and especially Communism (against whose members much Freikorps activity was directed). In order to shore up his shaky sense of self and autonomy, the male soldier constructs a "body armor" of rigid self-discipline that defends him against the temptations and vulnerability of sharing and pleasure and of sharing pleasure. These temptations and feelings of vulnerability, which were exacerbated by the humiliating defeat of Germany in the First World War and the Treaty of Versailles, can never be completely repressed, must be thrust out of the self and projected onto others, where they are relentlessly and ruthlessly hunted down for elimination. The Freikorps male psyche is therefore not that of an Oedipal neurotic, according to Theweleit, but a pre-Oedipal borderline psychotic, beset by the defense mechanism of splitting rather than that of symptom formation. Not only is the one-dimensionally "good" (white) woman categorically split off from the equally one-dimensional "bad" (red) woman (in a failure to synthesize good and bad objects central to the diagnostic repertoire of object-relations theory, on which Theweleit draws), but the male psyche itself radically splits off any feelings perceived as weak, joyous, sensuous, sinful, female, needy, commun(ion)al, contagious, fluid, and tempting; projects them onto outside others (usually women, but also Communists, Gypsies, Jews, etc.); and then sets out to punish and destroy those others in a frantic attempt to affirm the strength, virility, heroism, discipline, righteousness, superiority and independence of his own grandiose but unstable self-image.

Such a personality structure made it possible historically to first replace the red woman of fantasy with the flesh-and-blood Communists targeted by the Freikorps and slaughtered by the thousands, and then under Nazism to replace Communists with Jews, who were slaughtered by the millions. But it also makes it possible analytically to highlight similarities with the formation of the Ku Klux Klan during Reconstruction in the United States. In this instance, of course, the target was African Americans recently freed from slavery rather than Communists or Jews, and the founders were not German but Confederate officers who had themselves recently suffered a humiliating defeat in the Civil War and sought to pursue their lost cause by other means. For many whites who were not involved in the war itself, however, even the formal equality of African Americans was felt to be a humiliating defeat, and the Klan quickly spread beyond Civil War veterans. And although the first Klan was relatively short-lived, white supremacism would resurface in the twentieth and twenty-first centuries each time African Americans appeared to achieve greater degrees of parity with whites—most notably after the integration of American armed forces in the two World Wars, and then with the civil rights movement of the 1950s and '60s, followed by the election of a black president in 2008 (Chalmers 1987).

I turn finally to the psychodynamics of postwar American Christian supremacism, as distilled by Charles Strozier (1994) from hundreds of interviews of Christian "fundamentalists" conducted in New York City in the early 1990s. The personality structure of the Christian supremacist mirrors the Freikorps and Klan personalities in important respects. Where the latter were responding to humiliating military defeats, the dynamics of Christian supremacism revolve around the moment or process of conversion, the experience of being "born again" after "hitting bottom." Due to weak ego-synthetic abilities, Christian supremacists tend to see everything in stark, absolute terms of black and white, good versus evil. That a person, an object or a desire could involve a complex combination of positive and negative is something that they are unable or unwilling to allow. This leads to extreme tension between superego demands for absolute and unwavering adherence to a simplistic moral code on one hand, and multifarious drives and desires arising from the complexities and ambiguities of heterogeneous human existence in a mass-mediated global consumer society on the other—especially given the pressures to consume exorbitantly and define oneself in terms of sexuality. When such tensions become too great for a weak ego to bear, the psyche splits asunder: it cracks, and conversion occurs. Unacceptable drives and desires are categorized as sin and temptation and get split off and projected outward onto others; the ego identifies itself completely with the righteous authority of superego prohibitions. Relations with others henceforth take two characteristic forms, both serving to shore up an apparently grandiose but still fragile ego. For the most part, Christian supremacists tend to surround themselves with other fundamentalists just like themselves; in this way, they avoid having to think differently about themselves or to acknowledge split-off aspects of themselves that they might see in other, different people.[10] With respect to people who are indeed different from themselves, however, Christian supremacists will proselytize; and if those others fail to convert, they will be punished because they represent precisely those intolerable heterogeneous aspects of the fundamentalist psyche that brought on conversion in the first place. And in line with the psychodynamics of punitive projective identification, the severity of the punishment will correspond to the desperation with which the Christian supremacist seeks to maintain the self-righteous superego ideal over and against the temptations they constantly feel (and to which they often enough succumb): the greater the temptation, the harsher the punishment—projected onto others. For the beauty of projective splitting as a defense mechanism—insofar as it works—is that by exclusively targeting others, it lets the supremacists themselves off the hook. But of course, it doesn't work—or at least not for long. It is difficult enough to suppress human drives and desires completely in oneself, and it proves even more difficult—that is to say, impossible—to convert the entire world. Heterogeneity remains irreducible; no worldly solution appears possible. Absolutely committed to identification with a radically simplified version of Christianity, but unable of course to live or force others to live in accordance with fundamentalist strictures, the final solution is—apocalypse. Better to destroy a world considered to be irremediably steeped in sin than to accept almighty God's defeat by such a degraded and degrading world—a defeat that would also mean one's own. The fundamentalists interviewed by Strozier can become so self-righteous that, in fantasy at least, the ego's ultimate sacrifice to the superego culminates in extermination.

None of these specific historical examples of supremacism can be attributed directly to the capitalist market, of course. But there is another kind of borderline supremacism—what for want of a better term I will call "populist supremacism"—whose psychodynamic form is practically identical and whose content overlaps substantially with some of the historical instances outlined above. In populist supremacism, the sense of loss is occasioned not by military defeat or a fall into sin, but by capitalist austerity and the experience of precarity: the actual occurrence or ever-present threat of losing one's job and the ensuing loss of purchasing power, social standing, and market-mediated access to the means of life.[11] It is not only investment capitalists who can fall prey to the slope of the market if they don't outmatch the prevailing interest rates: consumers can fall out of the market, too, if they lose their jobs. Although capitalist austerity is the actual cause of such dispossession, populist supremacists target other vulnerable groups—immigrants, minorities, women, and others—for blame and retribution, often aligning their superego with that of a demagogue or other popular authority figure. Hence the considerable overlap between populist supremacism and other forms of borderline supremacism such as nativism, racism, and misogyny.[12]

Polymorphous Narcissism

Yet sacrificing the ego to intransigent superego ideals in this way is not the only possible response to the practically unavoidable conflict between multifarious drives and social conventions: there is a third permutation of the relations among id, ego, and superego. While the response of borderline supremacists lies closer to that of neurotics, who also sacrifice drive gratification to social convention, this third response lies closer to perversion, inasmuch as it involves siding with drive gratification against social convention. A generic coming-out narrative can provide a useful and dramatic illustration of this kind of response, especially in contrast with the Christian-supremacist conversion narrative examined above. Their points of departure are more or less the same: an excruciating and ultimately untenable conflict between certain desires and the social injunctions prohibiting them. But where the fragile born-again self aligns itself with a grandiose superego against the id, in line with the dynamics of psychic splitting and punitive projective identification, the embattled coming-out self allies itself with the id against external superego injunctions, struggling for the acceptance rather than the castigation of difference, while attempting to negotiate and indeed transform the conventional precepts of social authority regarding sexuality.

As suggestive as this contrast may be, it remains to be seen in what sense the psychodynamics at play in the coming-out narrative can be considered "narcissistic," especially given how widely definitions of narcissism vary.

Starting with Freud himself. In his earliest formulation (1914), narcissism was defined as a disorder involving the withdrawal of libido from objects to recathect the ego instead (1953, vol. 14). Even here, narcissism as a disorder was hypothesized to remobilize an earlier and perfectly normal "primary" narcissism based on the instinct of self-preservation; ego libido and object libido drew on the same reservoir of psychic energy, such that an increase in one would entail a decrease in the other. But in later works—notably *Civilization and Its Discontents* (1953, vol. 21) and *Future of an Illusion* (1953, vol. 21)—where the sexual and self-preservation instincts get replaced by the life and death drives, the concept of "primary narcissism" changes dramatically. (The disorder henceforth known as "secondary narcissism" remains basically unchanged.) Primary narcissism now refers to a developmental stage before the formation of the ego, before the emergence of the opposition between "subjective" and "objective," and before a sense of self with boundaries separating the self from others and the external world even exists. Rather than a libidinal cathexis of the self, primary narcissism designates the sensation of merging with the universe, rooted in the infantile experience of suckling blissfully at the mother's breast but extending beyond her body to encompass the entire universe. Freud describes this aspect of primary narcissism as an "oceanic feeling" of "an indissoluble bond, of being one with the external world as a whole" (1953, vol. 21, 65).

Psychoanalytically informed cultural criticism, too, varies considerably in its estimation of narcissism, depending on whether primary or secondary narcissism is foregrounded.[13] Richard Sennett (1974) and Christopher Lasch (1978, 1984), for example, base their criticism of American culture on the dynamics of secondary narcissism, which are also central to the analysis of borderline narcissism developed above.[14] For Marcuse (1955) and Brown (1959), however, primary narcissism is key: they propose that primary narcissism could provide the basis for a relationship to reality different from and superior to the reality principle as posited and undertheorized by Freud.[15]

For one thing, primary narcissism gives rise to an "ideal ego" whose primary drive remains the pursuit of pleasure, despite the renunciations called for by passage through the Oedipus complex. Specifically, the ideal ego refuses to accept a strict boundary between itself and the external world, refuses to completely sacrifice its "subjective" sense of reality to "objective" reality testing; in this respect, it lies closer to the psychotic pole of borderline conditions. For instead of accepting reality as given, the ideal ego retains a deeply-felt sense of connection to a not-yet or not-completely "external" world experienced as part of the self (and vice versa) rather than as standing over and against the self.[16] In object-relations terminology made famous by Melanie Klein and later adapted by Lacan and Deleuze and Guattari, the ideal ego experiences reality in the form of "partial objects" rather than whole objects.[17] Partial objects are partial in the dual sense that we are partial to them: we see them as sources of drive gratification, and that as such they are partial or incomplete: any "objective" qualities not conducive to gratification are ignored or considered inconsequential. The primary narcissism of the ideal ego construes the external world as a reflection of its needs and desires and construes objects of gratification as direct responses to or even extensions of embodied existence.

And the relation between this ideal ego and the "mature," post-Oedipal reality ego depends on the proportions in which the external world is experienced as a source of gratification and a source of frustration. That a bounded sense of self separate from an external world emerges at all is due to the experience of frustration and fledgling attempts to cope with it—at first through vocal activity (crying out to caregivers), and then increasingly through motor activity. Adequate care giving mitigates the degree of frustration and enables the gradual development of coping activities so that the integration of ideal ego and reality ego can take place relatively free of conflict. If, however, the degree of frustration is too great, or the disparity between gratification and frustration too drastic, the ideal ego gets submerged by the reality ego, and the latter clings desperately to its existing coping activities. This is one implication of Norman O. Brown's important corrective to Freud's famous dictum that "the instincts are innately conservative": if the ego resorts to the same old coping strategies, and if drives fixate on the same old objects, it is because the development of new ones is blocked by irremediable frustration and the ensuing repression of the death instinct because the reality ego doesn't experience enough integral gratification to let primitive coping activities die in favor of more developed ones. Neurosis is a classic instance of this kind of frustration-induced instinctual inertia, where the reality ego fixates on a relatively unobjectionable coping mechanism and its corresponding object, having been unable to develop more ideally gratifying ones. When the ideal ego retains its prerogatives vis-à-vis the reality ego, by contrast, the result is closer to perversion in that the commitment to drive gratification remains paramount—as the generic coming-out narrative clearly illustrates.

For the ideal ego as remnant of primary narcissism, the relation between self and world is primarily a matter of gratification.

While primary narcissism elevates or restores the strength of the ideal ego in relation to the reality ego, its effect on the proportionate strength of the ego ideal with respect to superego authority is similar. The rejection of social prohibitions (e.g., against same-sex love, as in the coming-out narrative) weakens the punitive component of the superego in favor of the ego ideal, whose central function is to furnish the ego with positive role models. Like the ideal ego, the ego ideal operates via a deeply felt connection with rather than separation from the ego; unlike obedience to superego prohibitions, ego-ideal emulation is based on shared rather than opposed values and on feelings of admiration rather than fear.

The decline of superego prohibitions has been attributed to the decline of paternal authority within the family, the argument being that the concentration of capital in fewer and fewer hands deprives the vast majority of men of any authority in the public sphere, which transfers to diminished authority in the domestic sphere. More widespread is the administration of social life by a growing number of bureaucracies: not only does each of them operate by formal rather than substantive rationality, therefore wielding power rather than venerable authority in its specialized domain, but their formal rationalities are independent of one another and therefore detract from rather than contribute to a coherent sense of authority valid for society as a whole. Finally, a society devoted principally to continually increasing the accumulation of surplus value by subordinating use value and meaning to exchange value is devoid of authority at its core, as Jonathan discovers in the climactic scene of *Rollerball*.

At the same time, mass-mediated global society offers a broader and broader array of role models to emulate. Access to the internet and the world market—through advertising if not actual purchases—enriches the imaginative hedonism of consumers with a welter of potentially admirable figures from around the globe. It also contributes to what I have called the "division of leisure" by enlarging and diversifying the set of available consumer goods and lifestyle choices along with the specialized tastes and/or skills required to enjoy them. Rather than eating for nourishment alone, for example, consumers are free to enjoy a variety of cuisines from around the world. In parallel with the multiplication of means of gratification, the now-global division of labor enlarges and diversifies the means of producing goods for the world market, further accelerating the development of specialized coping activities that began in infancy and continues throughout adulthood. These twin engines of specialization continually rewire the brain and enable people to produce and consume in new and differing ways, leading to what Marcuse and Brown propounded (each in his own way) as "polymorphous perversity."[18] And just as in childhood, the greater the success of these coping activities, and the more gratification in adulthood is achieved through them (or even convincingly promised), the more the polymorphous ideal ego connects narcissistically with its partial-object world and "perversely" diversifies its means of producing ever more gratification. Yet in the same vein, and conversely, the greater the frustration of adult coping activities and the less gratification is achieved through them, the more the precarious ego fixates on established (and to that extent neurotic) forms of gratification. And here, as the conclusions of *Mme. Bovary*, *Venus in Furs*, *Things*, and *Rollerball* amply demonstrate, it is not the father that is responsible for the frustration, but the interventions of the debt collector and the return more generally of capitalist austerity.

In this light, and in line with the priority of social determinations over familial ones, it is important to see borderline narcissism, borderline supremacism, and polymorphous narcissism not as discrete personality types, but rather as different tendencies or basins of attraction available in principle to any inhabitant of capitalist market society. And which tendency prevails will depend among other things on the historical conjuncture and the social position of the inhabitants in question: the greater the degree of frustration induced by capitalist austerity, the more likely and widespread the turn to borderline narcissism and borderline supremacism in some form; the greater the degree of gratification, the more likely and widespread the turn to polymorphous narcissism and the promotion of neurodiversity. The global explosions of freedom and creativity during the years of postwar prosperity known as "les trente glorieuses" and culminating in the 1960s aptly illustrate the latter, while the subsequent world-wide turn to populist nationalism in response to the austerity of neoliberal globalism in the early twenty-first century illustrates the former. In a similar vein, disaffected Civil War and German WW I veterans were prone to borderline supremacism, while Bohemians and students have for centuries been prone to primary narcissism and polymorphous perversity.

This positive form of perversity, distinct from the explicitly sexualized perversions examined in the previous chapter, is not just a result of overcoming scarcity and the performance principle (Marcuse) and of accepting separation and the death instinct (Brown): it lies at the core of market-mediated production and consumption. For perversity in this context refers to the turning away (Latin: *per-verto*) from concrete, qualitative, determinate value in favor of the abstract, quantitative, indeterminate value of money. Perversity in this sense, in other words, is an intrinsic effect of production for the market: goods are produced for sale rather than for immediate consumption. But perversity in this context thereby also means freedom from instinctual, traditional, and habitual determinations and greater freedom of choice among modes of gratification, as we have seen: market exchange just radically accelerates the vicissitudes to which human instincts are naturally prone. It thus becomes paramount to distinguish perversity in this special sense from the capitalist perversions because although production for the market is one hallmark of capitalism, not all markets are capitalist markets.[19] Even though perversity inheres in production for the market, not all production for the market is Sadistic, and not all forms of consumption are Masochistic: these perversions belong, as we have seen, specifically to the capitalist market.[20] I will return to this crucial distinction between perversity and perversion in the conclusion.

Part Two

Theoretical

Introduction

That historically variable social dynamics determine psychodynamics—rather than the other way around, as in Freudian psychoanalysis—is one of the basic premises of schizoanalysis, the "materialist psychiatry" Gilles Deleuze and Félix Guattari develop by critiquing Freud's ahistorical psychology using concepts from Marx and Nietzsche.[1] Deleuze and Guattari demonstrate the historical variability of social dynamics by comparing the capitalist mode of production with two earlier ideal-type modes of production, which they call "Savagery" and "Despotism." (As ideal types, they are capitalized, as is the figure of the Despot, who can be an emperor, king, or god; by contrast, capitalism—by which I mean Western capitalism—is considered a historical phenomenon and is therefore not capitalized.) This comparison reveals that capitalist society is based on market relations, which are meaningless, whereas previous societies were organized by meaningful codes (of conduct, social standing, etc.). Like *Rollerball*, then, schizoanalysis situates the existentialist tenet of the meaninglessness of human existence squarely in the context of capitalist social relations, which are based on what Deleuze and Guattari call "market axioms," rather than codes. Unlike social formations based on meaningful codes (of proper behavior, social standing, etc.), the fabric of capitalist society is knit by meaningless market axioms whose function is to conjoin quantified flows—flows of labor power and flows of liquid wealth, in the first instance, but also flows of technology, consumer taste, and so on—in order to produce surplus value for capital. Indeed, the most important cultural side effect of capitalist axioms is "decoding," which means not deciphering meaning to make it clearer, but, on the contrary, stripping away established meanings altogether—resulting at the limit in the kind of borderline schizophrenia illustrated by Roquentin's confrontation with the chestnut-tree root in *Nausea*. "Our [capitalist] society," Deleuze and Guattari insist, "produces schizos the same way it produces Prell shampoo or Ford cars" (1983, 245). And like Sartre, Deleuze and Guattari consider decoding to be an important vector of freedom, inasmuch as it frees experience from the weight of tradition and outmoded forms of understanding. Human beings, however, crave meaning, and operational social relations require it, so decoding is accompanied by subordinate processes of "recoding" that temporarily endow various regions of existence with at least the minimum local meanings needed for humans to be able to produce (job training), consume (marketing), and live together (culture). If decoding is responsible for the borderline conditions comprising the baseline of advanced capitalist psychodynamics, recoding designates myriad "meaningful" responses to it, including the three tendencies outlined at the end of the preceding chapter. Adapting another psychological term for sociohistorical analysis, Deleuze and Guattari characterize such meanings as "paranoid" inasmuch as the axioms that generate them as a by-product are themselves strictly meaningless. But like schizophrenia, paranoia occupies a spectrum: Sartre's "women in black" lie at one—relatively benign—end, while Theweleit's violent Nazi storm troopers lie at another. Generally speaking, the greater the degree of deprivation—of meaning, social standing, and/or means of life—the greater the degree of paranoia, as evidenced by borderline supremacists' remarkable susceptibility to paranoid conspiracy theories. In this context, polymorphous narcissism stands out as a notable exception, inasmuch as it generates meanings that are partial and maintains a sense of connection rather than deprivation. Chapter 4 will explore how such radically different responses to the meaningless axioms of capitalism are possible.

In developing an analytic framework adequate to the complex dynamics of capitalist axiomatization, Deleuze and Guattari proceed by critically adapting selected components of concepts from mathematics (the primary source of axiomatic theory), political economy, and psychoanalysis, while ignoring or critiquing others. With respect to Freud, for example, schizoanalysis adapts his concepts of libido and the repetition compulsion but critiques the Oedipus complex and the death instinct as insufficiently historical. The relation of schizoanalysis to Marx's critique of political economy is similar (though less explicitly thematized in Deleuze and Guattari's works than the relation to

Freud); here what is most notable is the shift in focus from capital itself to the capitalist market that takes place between the first and second volumes of *Capitalism and Schizophrenia*. Although near the beginning of the second volume Deleuze and Guattari insist that "RHIZOMATICS=SCHIZOANALYSIS= STRATOANALYSIS=PRAGMATICS=MICROPOLITICS" (1987, 22), later concepts differ in important ways from earlier ones.[2] Schizophrenia, the erstwhile psychological term central to *Anti-Oedipus*, practically disappears in *A Thousand Plateaus* and gives way instead to concepts of nomadism and the war machine, which emphasize social and spatial relations rather than internal psychodynamics.[3] At the same time, their use of the concept of axiomatics is extended from economics (the axioms of capital) to law and science, thereby warding off the charge of what Anna Kornbluh (2019) calls "anarcho-vitalism," which might have been leveled at the first volume.[4] Even more importantly, capital is no longer considered the "full body" or "socius" that appropriates productive forces in the capitalist mode of production: it is construed as an "apparatus of capture" (1987, plateau 13) that is grafted onto the market, instead. And what it captures is not just labor power, but also purchasing power (Karatani 2003; Dick and McLaughlan 2020), attention (Zuboff 2019), service connectivity (Srnicek 2016), bioreflexes (Ward 2022), subjectivity (Read 2003; Tomšič 2015), the reproductive forces of nature (Cooper 2008; Moore 2015), and the commons (Casarino and Negri 2008; Hardt and Negri 2009; Bensaid 2014)—thereby enabling schizoanalysis to address recent developments of capitalism better than a focus on labor power alone.[5] Replacing capital with the market and "defining social formations by *machinic processes* rather than modes of production" (1987, 435; original emphasis) also enable Deleuze and Guattari to argue that the capitalist market can profit from a wide variety of productive processes spread across the globe that are themselves not capitalist in nature.[6] Nor are they construed as holdovers fated for eventual elimination in a linear history of modernization: they "*certainly do not constitute vestiges or transitional forms,*" but if anything could be considered "ultramodern" (1987, 435; original emphasis). Perhaps most dramatically, what Deleuze and Guattari in their later works consider "universal" is no longer history, as per *Anti-Oedipus*, but the world market itself—which is "the only thing," they conclude in their final collaboration, "that is universal in capitalism" (1994, 106). Hence the importance of showing what capital does to markets, as I have done in part 1 regarding the psychodynamics of Sadism and Masochism. To better understand how they reach this conclusion, I explain in chapter 3 why it is so important to supplement Freud's analysis of the psychodynamics of the nuclear family with an analysis of the psychodynamics of the capitalist market and then turn in chapter 4 to explain how the capitalist market functions as an open axiomatic system.

There are limitations, however, to Deleuze and Guattari's perspective. The most troubling is their use of axiomatic and set theory terminology from mathematics, which as Jon Roffe (2015; 2016) has shown can be extremely misleading. The solution adopted here—also proposed by Roffe (2016, 149)—is to create a philosophical concept of axiomatics rather than claim to be using mathematical theory literally.[7] Philosophy treats concepts as part objects or multiplicities rather than essences: components of a concept that help illuminate a given problem are retained while those that don't are selected out.[8] To develop a properly philosophical concept of capitalist axiomatics, I will for example retain the distinction between denumerable and nondenumerable sets, without being concerned with the relative size of various infinite sets.

The point of examining in depth the psychodynamics of market relations and the sociodynamics of axiomatization is to show how the capitalist market fosters both perversion and perversity and what the potential advantages and actual disadvantages are of having the market serve as the very basis of social organization. But in addition to the implications of axiomatics for social organization and politics, there are important implications for philosophy and other forms of thought. For Deleuze and Guattari argue (1994, especially chapter 4) that philosophy has truly flourished in two specific historical epochs, that it emerged and then reemerged in connection with two distinctive social milieus: first the Greek city-state, and now global capitalism. In both cases, what is especially propitious for philosophical thought is its connection to a social milieu that includes a self-organizing multiplicity. In the case of the ancient Greek city-state, it is the *agora* that functions as a self-organizing multiplicity: it brings together citizens as friends and rivals and most importantly as equals, among whom there is (in principle) no preestablished social hierarchy and hence no transcendent authority figure; authority arises immanently from discussion itself, instead. In this case, the multiplicity is political. The case of global capitalism is more complicated, but here it is the world market that functions as the self-organizing multiplicity. Market exchange coordinates the conjugation of flows of all kinds, while axiomatization decodes meaning and hence subverts centralized social authority. In this case, then, the multiplicity is economic rather than political. In both cases, what is key is the kind of relation that thought entertains with its social milieu.

Unlike science, which strives to represent aspects of the world as it actually is, philosophy is creative and serves as a kind of relay between one practical orientation to the world and another, new (and hopefully improved) one. Philosophy responds to problems that arise when a given mode of existence or practical orientation no longer suffices. Such problems are real enough, but they are not reducible to reality. The purpose of philosophy is not to represent the world, but to create concepts and what Deleuze and Guattari (1994, chapter 3) call "conceptual personae," whose purpose is not to accurately replicate in discourse specific segments of the world as it really is (as science does), but to propose articulations of and/or solutions to problems, to offer new and different perspectives on or orientations toward the world. Take for example the problem facing Greek society, as Plato construes it: emergent democracy fosters free speech and through its exercise, Sophists threaten to undermine hierarchical social order; his solution: the conceptual persona called "Socrates," who will invent a practice of the dialectic to engage with and "correct" immanent public opinion in the interests of a transcendent Truth, becoming thereby a cornerstone of state philosophy (and hence a constant target of Deleuze and Guattari's nomad thought). Plato is, on one hand, a prodigious creator of concepts (the Socratic dialectic, the Ideal Forms, etc.) and of conceptual personae (not just the figure of Socrates, but also the philosopher-king, the guardians, and others). The dialogues contain, on the other hand, numerous points of contact with reality: nascent democracy, the agora, the Sophists, Socrates himself, and so on. The conceptual persona "Socrates" is derived from Socrates the person and his particular social milieu; but it does not represent him or that milieu. Even if there are features of the historical milieu that resemble concept-formations in philosophy (features such as the real-life Sophists and Socrates) the "corresponding" conceptual persona or philosophical concept (Socrates or the dialectic, for example) does not represent those psychosocial types: "Conceptual personae are irreducible to psychosocial types. . . . Nietzsche's Dionysus is no more the mythical Dionysus than Plato's Socrates is the historical Socrates" (1994, 67, 65). In much the same vein, Deleuze and Guattari insist in *Anti-Oedipus* (1983, 380) that "they have never seen a schizophrenic"—despite the fact that the schizophrenic as conceptual persona is in a sense the very hero of the book (though not its only conceptual persona). The point is that the conceptual persona of the "schizo" is a completely different kind of entity from the flesh-and-blood schizophrenic: "In one case the schizophrenic is a conceptual persona who lives intensely within the thinker and forces him to think, whereas in the other the schizophrenic is a psychosocial type who represses the living being and robs him of his thought" (1994, 70).

So, the connection between philosophical thought and its sociohistorical milieu is essentially diagnostic rather than representative-scientific: "All concepts are connected to problems without which they would have no meaning and which can themselves only be isolated or understood [as problems] as their solution emerges" (1994, 16). Sciences aim to grasp states of affairs as they are; the point is to get reality right, to settle on a correct understanding of the world. Philosophy aims never to settle but on the contrary always to unsettle and to transform our understanding of certain problems because they are thought to have been badly posed, or not posed at all, by previous thinkers, and/or because the problems are historically new or have changed so radically over time as to render previous responses inadequate. Hence Deleuze and Guattari insist that philosophy for them "does not consist in knowing and is not inspired by truth. Rather it is categories like Interesting, Remarkable, or Important that determine [its] success or failure" (1994, 82). The creation of concepts is thus crucially selective as well as (or as part of being) diagnostic; philosophy selects out from states of affairs "what belongs by right to thought and only to thought" (1994, 69; see also 37 and 50–52). And in extracting a philosophical concept from a historical state of affairs, thought chooses certain determinations as "Interesting, Remarkable, or Important," and "relegates other determinations to the status of mere facts, characteristics of states of affairs, or lived contents" (1994, 52). The concept of schizophrenia, for instance, gets created through the extraction of selected features from a historical state of affairs characterized by the spread of the world market, the subversion of meaning by axiomatization, and the resulting prospects for a radically free "infinite semiosis" at play throughout society.

The diagnostic function of thought is not limited to philosophy, however: literature, too, can be diagnostic—as the works of Sade and Masoch (but also Sophocles and others) make perfectly clear. Indeed, Deleuze and Guattari derive their concept of schizophrenia from works of literature (by Artaud, Beckett, et al.) as much as from psychoanalysis or psychiatry.[9] But here we encounter another limitation of Deleuze's work. As essential as his study of Sadean and Masochean discourse in *Coldness and Cruelty* (1971) was to the historical analysis in part 1, his aim there was to dispel the supposed symmetry between sadism and masochism as defined by sexology by showing that each is in fact a discrete syndrome in its own right, and not simply the inverse of the other. It is, as Deleuze avows (1971, 14–16), an exercise in symptomatology and shows the authors themselves to be great symptomatologists. But it doesn't go so far as to treat them as diagnosticians nor make clear what the object of their diagnoses might be. Only later, in what Daniel W. Smith (Deleuze 1997, xi) calls his "*critique et clinique* project," will Deleuze insist (but without referencing Sade and Masoch) that what the best literary works diagnose is not individual psychology but syndromes characteristic of the culture at large: "Authors, if they are great, are more like doctors than patients," writes Deleuze (following Nietzsche): "They are clinicians of civilization" (1990, 237; 1997, xvii).[10] And instead of operating via concepts, literature operates as a kind of experimental ethics, by inventing fictional modes of existence (fictional rather than conceptual personae) that are then subject to ethical evaluation by authors and readers alike.[11] Philosophical reading can then extract from fictional personae various critical concepts, such as (but not limited to) the concepts of Sadism and Masochism I have developed here. That is one reason why not just obviously diagnostic works such as Sade's and Masoch's but less obviously diagnostic works ranging from *Native Son* to *Nausea* to *Rollerball* can be mobilized to help diagnose the culture of capitalism.[12] What intolerable problems—such as Sadism or Masochism—does a given literary work select from its social milieu as particularly "Interesting, Remarkable, or Important"? And conversely, what positive tendencies does it identify in the social milieu—such as decoding and polymorphous narcissism—that might serve as potential solutions to those (and/or other) problems? As part 1 has shown, great works of philosophy and literature enable us to diagnose the capitalist market as the source of both intolerable perversion and subjugation, on one hand, and potential polymorphous perversity and enhanced freedom, on the other. The challenge is to generate and experiment with ways to eliminate the former and foster the latter. The conclusion will show why salvaging the market from capitalism is essential to achieving those results.

Chapter Three

The Psychodynamics of the Capitalist Market

Always historicize!

—Fredric Jameson, *The Political Unconscious*

Schizoanalysis completes and revolutionizes the psychoanalytic project by restoring to it the critical thrust it lost with the adoption of the life/death-instinct model and by linking it to social transformation rather than individual therapy alone. It accomplishes this transformation by situating the psychodynamics of the family (Freud) and of language or representation (Lacan) in the context of the capitalist market, whose sociodynamics have superseded and absorbed the sociodynamics of Savagery and Despotism. But speaking of psychodynamics and sociodynamics as if they were separate from one another is misleading: according to Deleuze and Guattari, they are in fact the same dynamic, which appears to operate in two distinct registers because of the segregation of the nuclear family from society at large under capitalism.[1] The privatization of reproduction in the domestic sphere parallels the privatization of the fruits of production in the public sphere. Even speaking in favor of introjection rather than projection, as I have done above, belies the fundamental identity of psycho- and sociodynamics.[2]

Deleuze and Guattari's critique of Freudian psychoanalysis targets not one but two of its key concepts: not only the Oedipus complex (as per the title of the first volume of *Capitalism and Schizophrenia: Anti-Oedipus*), but also the death instinct. Significantly, both concepts are targeted not for being simply wrong, but for being insufficiently historical. It's not that Freud completely misunderstood the Oedipus complex and the death instinct, in other words, but that he refused to recognize them as features belonging specifically to capitalist society. In fact, Freud explicitly acknowledged that Reich's critique of the death instinct (on which Deleuze and Guattari draw) as ahistorical and apolitical meant, as Freud himself put it, that "what we call the death instinct is a product of the capitalist system" (Jones 1960 vol. 3, 166; quoted in Noyes 1997, 194); but he dismissed Reich's views and insisted on treating the Oedipus complex and the death instinct as universal features of the human psyche. Hence the importance of historicizing Freudian concepts by resituating them in the context of capitalism, with the ulterior aim of revealing the social determinations of two main forms of anxiety identified by psychoanalysis: castration anxiety and separation anxiety. Schizoanalysis prosecutes the historicization of Freud by means of two analytic procedures: contrasting capitalism with other social formations to highlight their very different treatments of death and expenditure and comparing the nuclear family with the capitalist economy to highlight their very similar structures and dynamics.[3]

In sharp contrast to its subordinate status in precapitalist social forms, the market under capitalism has become the very foundation of society, superseding (yet without eliminating) the interpersonal and political relations that formed the basis of previous societies. Hence the peculiar mixture under capitalism of apparent freedom (from directly personal and political forms of subordination) and actual enslavement (to the capitalist market itself, in the forms of wage slavery and what can be called "return-on-investment" slavery). With the advent of the capitalist market, social representation has changed regime: "Representation no longer relates to a distinct object, but to productive activity itself," inasmuch as commodified labor power has become the measure of market value (Deleuze and Guattari 1983, 263). This shift from objective to subjective evaluation in economics explains the importance to schizoanalysis of one of Freud's key insights: that similar to economic value, erotic value does not inhere in objects but depends instead on the vicissitudes of subjective investment (libido). Following Foucault's analysis of the evolution of psychology from classical psychiatry to psychoanalysis, then, Deleuze and Guattari argue that "Freud is the Luther and the Adam Smith of psychiatry" for just as Luther and Smith determined that the essence of religion and wealth lay not in gods or money but in the abstract subjective essence of interior religiosity and of production in general (respectively), Freud determines that the essence of desire is not to be found in its objects or aims, but in an abstract subjective essence—libido or sexuality in general (Deleuze and Guattari 1983, 271; see also 299–300, 303). But having determined the de-coded essence of desire as abstract libido, Freud (like Luther and Smith) then re-codes that subjective essence onto the nuclear family with its Oedipus complex (just as they re-territorialize subjective religiosity onto scripture and abstract labor onto capital). The twin aims of revolutionary schizoanalysis will therefore be to free desire from Oedipus and to free labor-power from capital, based on an analysis that situates Oedipal-familial psychodynamics in the context of the psychodynamics of the capitalist market.

Structure and Dynamics of the Nuclear Family and Capital

Schizoanalysis identifies the nuclear family as a capitalist institution. In no other social formation is the biological and psychological reproduction of individuals so widely and thoroughly segregated from the collective reproduction of social relations, and the family reduced to a narrowed kinship structure where relations of filiation are limited to only two generations—parents and children, to the exclusion of grandparents—and relations of alliance are limited to siblings—brothers and sisters, to the exclusion of uncles, aunts, and cousins (Poster 1978). In effect, the privatization of reproduction in the nuclear family mirrors the privatization of accumulation in the hands of capital.

But this is more than a structural homology: the family triangle serves in effect as a relay by imprinting the psychodynamics of the capitalist market on individuals from the moment of their birth: "Father, mother, and child thus become the simulacrum of the images of capital ('Mister Capital, Madame Earth,' and their child the Worker), with the result that . . . familial determinations become the application of the social axiomatic" (Deleuze and Guattari 1983, 264). Just as capital separates the worker from the means of life (via the dispossession of so-called primitive accumulation) and defers gratification until after work, after payday, and after retirement, the castrating Father separates the child from the nurturing Mother (via the so-called incest taboo) and defers gratification until maturity and the founding of a new family. As with respect to the work of Norman O. Brown in part 1, the principle of deferred action (*Nachträglickheit*) reveals the social determinations of castration anxiety: it is the threat to one's livelihood represented by working for—and hence always potentially getting fired by—a boss that retroactively endows family relations with an especially traumatic surcharge. But here, that charge resonates with childhood circumstances that are themselves already traumatic, given the peculiar segregation and narrowed structure of the capitalist nuclear family: all the nearest objects of desire are taboo, and it is a taboo that the Father as representative of social authority (in patriarchal society) is delegated to enforce. The punitive authority and monopoly on enjoyment once belonging to the Despot migrate into the family unit and now belong to the Father or the Father function. The capitalist nuclear family thus proves to be an ideal relay and training ground for docile obedience and asceticism: Oedipalized workers who were already accustomed to being denied the objects of their desire by the structure of the nuclear family and the castrating authority of the Father are all the better prepared to tolerate being denied the fruits of their labor by the structure of capital and to obey the castrating authority of the boss. Then, in a further historical development, the psychodynamics of the nuclear family undergo an important modification. The locus of authority, as we have seen, shifts from Father to Mother within the private, domestic sphere, where a Masochistic regime of imaginative hedonism and endless, self-fulfilling consumerism prevails in compensation for the obedience and self-denial still required at work. Asceticism and hedonism come to coexist uneasily in a family-sponsored "split personality" that internalizes the increasing distance between production and consumption fostered by the capitalist market.[4]

Not only is the nuclear family a capitalist institution, but so in a sense is the so-called incest taboo—that is, the taboo in the negative or prohibitive formulation we are most familiar with ("thou shall not sleep with mother or sisters"). For Savage societies with extended family forms or clans, the social imperative is not negative, but positive; it is a prescription rather than a proscription: thou shall forge kinship relations with members of other extended families or clans. Indeed, the entire social fabric in such societies is knit by precisely such kinship relations, and the imperative to share applies to the fruits of the hunt as well as the fruits of the womb: the results of production and reproduction alike cannot be privately consumed, but must rather circulate throughout the community, distributed according to a patchwork of mobile and dischargeable debts. In pre-capitalist Despotic or state societies, the social imperative is mixed: immediate consumption or expenditure of the fruits of production and reproduction is denied to the Despot's subjects because it is permissible for and monopolized by the Despot himself. The patchwork of reciprocal and dischargeable debts characteristic of Savage society has become a unilateral debt to the Despot that can never be discharged, and that can therefore be considered infinite, albeit in a very particular sense I will return to below.

It is in capitalist societies, finally, that the social imperative has become purely negative, a real (and well-nigh biological) taboo: nuclear family members are proscribed by the so-called incest taboo, and there is no correlative positive prescription. Under capitalism, kinship relations (such as they exist) remain a purely private matter: the social fabric is knit neither by relations of kinship (as in Savagery) nor by relations of public fealty (as in Despotism), but by the axioms of the capitalist market. And the unilateral debt now owed to capital is if anything even more infinite than the debt once owed to the Despot—and this for three reasons. Although the Despot had the power of life and death over his subjects, they only owed him their death, if they disobeyed, not their life; and the amount they did owe was over and above the means of life they collectively produced and consumed for themselves. The subjects of capitalism, by contrast, owe capital their whole lives, and rather than "taking" those lives, capital makes them as productive and reproductive as possible. What's more, unlike Despotic subjects who consume means of life they have produced for themselves, capitalist subjects are completely dependent on the market for their means of life. Even more important: whereas the Despot's expenditure of the material wealth derived from in-kind tribute payments has physical and physiological limits, the accumulation of surplus value generated by capitalist production and consumption has none and can be pursued to infinity. Unlike substantial wealth, the accumulation of value in liquid form has literally no end—in both senses of the term.[5] The transition from Despotism to capitalism is thus characterized by the subordination of the state—the central institution of Despotism—to the process of market axiomatization—the basic operation of capitalism. The Despotic State exercised power by monopolizing expenditure for the greater glory of the Despot. The capitalist State, by contrast, exercises power merely so as to assure suitable conditions for the social production and private accumulation of surplus value.

There are thus three key features of the transition from despotism to capitalism: the replacement of the figure and administration of the Despot by the capitalist market as the basis of social relations; the subordination of the state to the imperatives of capital accumulation; and the migration of the figure of the Despot into the heart of the nuclear family in the figure of the castrating Father, which translates what had been the noisy, socially imposed terror of despotism into the silent, privatized, self-generating Oedipal guilt of modern capitalism.⁶ Freud misrecognizes the historical migration of patriarchal authority from the objective social relations of despotism to the subjective familial relations of capitalism; indeed, to provide further evidence for his universalizing psychology, he substitutes projection for migration in his analysis of the representations of the Oedipus complex found in myth and tragedy: he is happy to consider them as further evidence for the universality of his psychology but ultimately must treat them all as so many projections onto various external media of the strictly internal fantasy life of Oedipal man.⁷ With the capitalist market's decoding of social authority and objective social representations, we no longer really believe in myth and tragedy, but psychoanalysis restores our belief in the Oedipus by converting it from an objective into a subjective representation. "Psychoanalysis undoes [myth and tragedy] as objective representations, and discovers in them the figures of a subjective universal libido; but it re-animates them, and promotes them as subjective representations that extend the mythic and tragic contents [of Oedipus] to infinity" (Deleuze and Guattari 1983, 304). In short, psychoanalysis decodes Oedipus as determinate objective representation but then recodes it as infinite subjective representation.

To understand why Deleuze and Guattari characterize subjective representation as "infinite" and consider the modern mode of repression so much more noxious than those of Savagery and Despotism, we need only review the status and role of debt in the three social formations analyzed by Deleuze and Guattari. Whereas in Savagery the debt is finite and reciprocal and the risk of death transient, they become permanent and unidirectional under Despotism: everyone owes the Despot everything, including their death, which hangs over their existence in the form of omnipresent terror. The debt to the Despot appears infinite, but as a transcendent figure he nonetheless represents what Foucault calls the "limit of the Limitless": because he takes human or anthropomorphic form and because his subjects can owe him no more than their death, the apparently infinite debt has limits (Foucault 1977, 32). But when the quantitative calculus of the capitalist market displaces the Despot as the basis of social relations in capitalism, those limits disappear: infinity, as we saw in chapter 1, has become properly mathematical rather than figural, an impersonal calculation rather than a personal limit.⁸ Moreover, capitalist subjects owe more than their deaths, as we have seen: they owe their very lives, and all that modern, productive biotechnopower can make out of human life. The modern, internalized form of infinite debt is now incalculable and has become truly endless. Modern power represses desire not negatively, by restraining or prohibiting it, but "positively" or constructively, by capturing it, stimulating, and enhancing it, as we have seen, so as to continually increase surplus production and continue to pay the infinite debt to capital (Lazzarato 2015; Di Muzio and Robbins 2016). The Despot as "limit of the Limitless" has succumbed to the "limitless reign of the Limit," as Foucault characterizes it (1977, 32), inasmuch as the infinite calculus of capital continually displaces its own limit.[9]

As capital and the "cash nexus" of the capitalist market displace the Despot as the basis of social relations and market decoding undermines all objective social representations, the locus of authority shifts to the nuclear family, where subjective representations prevail in the place of objective ones. The ultimate source of these representations is still the social formation at large, but the first locus of application of these subjective representations is the enclave of the nuclear family, segregated from the rest of society and therefore sheltered from the implacable mechanisms of decoding that operate there. This is why subjective representation is indeterminate as well as infinite: subjective representations under capitalism are mere "images of images," relayed ultimately from the social formation but via the mediation of the nuclear family, where they acquire all sorts of peculiar idiosyncratic or familiosyncratic overdeterminations.[10] Individuals beset by the discontents of civilization are nonetheless constituted and trapped by Oedipal-familial images and end up struggling with their private demons and intimate Despots instead of fighting against true social ills and economic injustice.

It is no wonder, in this light, that Deleuze and Guattari consider the capitalist pacification of libido so much more virulent and paralyzing than even the terror of Despotism. Endless capital accumulation systemically subordinates expenditure and enjoyment to surplus production, thereby suffusing the entire economy with death in disguise and making the instincts appear conservative. Representative images (of, e.g., gratification, exertion, deferral, interdiction, etc.) themselves derived from social functions (consumption, work, accumulation, etc.) are relayed into the family, where they constitute the very subjectivity of modern subjects. For a regime of unending accumulation, the repayment of an infinite debt sponsors a regimen of everlasting guilt: the Oedipal internalization of that infinite debt via the intermediary of the nuclear family and all its taboos. Passage through the Oedipus complex comes to appear necessary as the only way to curb death, now construed as an instinct, by turning it against itself. And the problem with most Freudian theory is that it actually reinforces the capitalist pacification of libido in the name of a universal psychology and with its projection paradigm relieves capital of all responsibility.

The schizoanalytic prioritization of social dynamics over psychodynamics not only exposes the nuclear family and the Freudian Oedipus complex as relays for the reproduction of docile capitalist subjects; it also and more importantly reveals that Oedipal-familial recoding is the subordinate tendency of capitalist axiomatization.[11] Decoding is the predominant tendency, and by freeing difference and semiotic free play from the constraints of social codes, by promoting schizophrenia as freedom, and by radically expanding the variability of modes of gratification to which human instincts are naturally prone, market decoding makes history universal, not psychology. To the extent that axiomatization generates more differences than it can recode and recapture in standard-model identities, capital functions as a "difference-engine" (Ansell-Pearson, 1997). It thus stands alongside the other major difference engines, biological evolution and linguistic expression, all of which achieve enhanced capacity through the articulation of difference and operate according to the universal processes of differentiation and consolidation—the diastole and systole of the cosmos, in Deleuze's colorful turn of phrase (Deleuze 2004, 29–30, 37). In the case of life, random mutation produces differences, from which ecological selection then consolidates organs and species; in the case of language, infinite semiosis produces differential relations among both signifiers and signifieds, from which expression consolidates signs. In the case of capital, the divisions of labor and leisure generate an increasingly differentiated multiplicity of specialized jobs and tastes along with enhanced capacities for creation and enjoyment, which the market now articulates for the production of value and the accumulation of capital but could articulate for the production of wealth and the enhancement of life, instead. And the key to this alternative is the process of axiomatization, the subject of chapter 4.

Death and Enjoyment

Deleuze and Guattari's critique of Freud's death instinct is both political and historical. The political charge is straightforward enough: it's that, in Freud's theorization, the death instinct (which he substituted relatively late in his career for the earlier instinct model involving self-preservation and reproduction) replaces social repression as the source of anxiety and thus absolves civilization of all liability for the discontents it visits on its members. The historical charge is perhaps less dramatic, and certainly more complicated, for Freud's formulation is shown to express or reflect quite accurately the way death functions *under capitalism*. And this is where the historical critique rejoins a broader political one: in its concept of the death instinct (as in the Oedipus complex), Freudian theory merely reflects and reinforces the "apparent objective movement" of capital.[12] Deleuze and Guattari will thus insist (1983, 130, 133, 299, 310) on "leading psychoanalysis to the point of its autocritique" by identifying—and condemning—the way death functions in the psychodynamics of capitalism as well as, by extension or reflection, in Freudian psychoanalysis itself.

The principal function of death in so-called primitive or Savage society is to confer superior social standing—what Marcel Mauss (2002) would call "prestige" and Georges Bataille (1988) would call "sovereignty"—on those who demonstrate that they can face death directly. Social life revolves around public rituals (such as the "potlatch" analyzed by Mauss) in which the risk of death is proudly confronted and sovereignty is achieved by anyone willing to divest themselves of the means of life, whether by giving them away to others or simply by destroying them. By contrast, the risk of death willingly undertaken in turn by various social actors in recurrent Savage rituals becomes in Despotic or state society a permanent threat of death at the command of the ruling Despot. And, as Foucault (1979) has shown, the Despotic reign of terror certainly entails, and may even depend on, very public ritual displays of capital punishment and torture sponsored by the Despot to assert and reinforce sovereign power over his subjects. It would be quite difficult to maintain, as Freud does, that death is always and everywhere a "silent instinct," in light of its very different and very public roles in pre-capitalist societies such as these.

Death functions differently in modern, capitalist society. Instead of being openly confronted as a means of conferring social standing or publicly mobilized to instill fear of the Despot's wrath, death is either (1) projected outside of the modern nation-state in the form of war against other nation-states; (2) hidden away in the bowels of prisons, in the rare instances that it is still allowed as a form of punishment, where it is visible only to a limited number of select state witnesses; or (3) prevented or delayed as long as possible by bringing to bear on it all the resources of medicine, hygiene, nutrition, exercise, and so on. In an economy driven by the imperative constantly to produce and accumulate more and more surplus value, killing potential producer-consumers is utterly inefficient and irrational. Foucault (2004a) penned an incisive catchphrase to sum up the contrasting functions of death in Despotic and capitalist society: in the former, the rule is "let live and make die," while in the latter, it is "make live and let die." The Despot was content to let people live more or less as they wish, but he would make them die if they disobeyed him or represented a threat to his power. Capital, by contrast, will make people live so that they can produce surplus value; will simply let them die if they do not do so; and if they disobey, would prefer in most cases to rehabilitate rather than execute them so that they can return to the workforce as productive citizens. In an economy devoted to endless accumulation, then, death no longer has an avowed social function—at least not on the top side of the market, the side governed by the imperatives of capital. On the underside of the market, however, the fear of being left to die, the condition now often referred to as "precarity," is very real: anyone without gainful employment will be unable to purchase means of life, which for all intents and purposes are available only on the market—and will thereby be left to die. This very real fear is one of the primary social determinations of separation anxiety under capitalism.

Contrasting capitalist and precapitalist societies reveals another difference between them regarding the treatment of means and ends. The glory of enhanced social standing attained by the public expenditure of means of life (resources) is the end to which all precapitalist societies are devoted, whether such glory is shared in turn by various members of Savage society or gets monopolized in Despotism by the Despot at the expense of his tribute-paying subjects (Mauss 2002; Deleuze and Guattari 1983, chapter 3). In capitalist society, however, public expenditure is scorned and severely curtailed for the sake of perpetual private accumulation: capitalist production is undertaken primarily to produce more capital for reinvestment in further production. In other words, the primary "end" of production under capitalism is, paradoxically enough, the endless production of more means (of production: capital). There is a secondary aim of capitalist production, it is true, and this secondary aim does involve expenditure and enjoyment: this is the privatized form of expenditure known as consumption or consumerism. But as we have seen, consumerism is Masochistic, inasmuch as private expenditure on the capitalist market ends up increasing the power of capital over social life by making ever more liquid funds available to capitalists for reinvesting in further means of appropriating surplus value and securing the legal and political means to continue doing so (e.g., buying legislators and judges). So, the ultimate end of both production and consumption under capitalism is the endless production of means. This capitalist substitution of means for ends is itself a form of perversion: the imperative to accumulate rather than enjoy amounts literally to turning away (Latin: *per-vertere*) from ends to focus instead on means, amounts to turning away from the social production and collective enjoyment of wealth to invest instead in the social production and private accumulation of surplus value.

But the capitalist market affects the relations between means and ends in another way, as well. The feature of capitalism identified by Lukács (1971a) as reification leads to the predominance in Weber's terms of formal over substantive rationality: it becomes increasingly difficult for people to devise their own means to achieve their ends because in an administered society, to recall Marcuse's (1964, 1969) term, the means are controlled by bureaucratic institutions operating according to a gamut of disparate formal rationalities. In the terms Deleuze (1986) adapted from Bergson, the customary sensory-motor schema that would ordinarily lead more or less immediately from the identification of a desired result in a given situation to a course of action to achieve that result have been disrupted by the intermediation of institutionalized formal rationalities. Action in the public sphere then gets replaced by feeling and imagination in the private sphere, typified in the imaginative hedonism of Masochistic consumerism, as we saw in chapter 1.

The capitalist market has yet another impact on the relations between means and ends, which is no doubt the most important. One of the prerequisites for the emergence and continuation of capitalism is the process Marx (1975, vol. 1, part 8) refers to as "so-called primitive accumulation." He adds the skeptical epithet ("so-called") to the bourgeois political economists' category of "primitive accumulation" in order to stress that the key feature of this process is not really an accumulation of liquid wealth ready to be invested as capital (as necessary as this may be), but rather the forced separation of workers from their means of life. Equally important: the process of so-called primitive accumulation is not limited to the moment of emergence of capitalism but is crucial to capital's ongoing and requisite self-expansion. Indeed, the dispossession of workers (Harvey 2005a) to make them both dependent on capital for gainful employment and dependent on the capitalist market for the goods with which to sustain themselves remains the cornerstone of the capitalist mode of production, inasmuch as labor power and purchasing power are the primary sources of surplus value.[13] And it is this precarious dependency that triggers or aggravates what psychoanalysis calls "separation anxiety." Dependency and separation anxiety are central themes in the universalizing account Freud gives of childhood development: through birth and then weaning, everyone eventually separates from their dependence on nourishment from the Mother's placenta and breasts, and the separation process can induce anxiety for being either too fast or too slow. But here again the Freudian principle of deferred action (*Nachträglichkeit*) bears fruit: it is the precarious dependence of adults on a capitalist market devoted primarily to accumulating means rather than to enjoying ends that retroactively endows separation with traumatic charge, whether the process in childhood was too fast, too slow, or just right. Such is the social overdetermination of separation anxiety by the capitalist market.

Now the principal psychic effect of aggravated anxiety of any kind, according to psychoanalysis, is neurotic fixation on the past, which seems to guarantee satisfaction in the face of anxiety. In the terms of *Difference and Repetition* (Deleuze 1994, especially 16–25 and 287–90), neurotic fixation reduces the proportion of difference in repetition to a minimum, whereas schizophrenia, as defined in *Anti-Oedipus* (Deleuze and Guattari 1983), maximizes the proportion of difference in repetition. Instead of continually developing new ways of satisfying drives, the neurotic constantly reverts to the same old form of substitute gratification. Perversion shares the same structure with neurosis, except that while the sexual nature of the substitute symptom is disguised in neurosis, it remains obvious in perversion. In both cases, instead of satisfaction being achieved by repeating with a difference in the future whatever is found to be pleasurable in the present, satisfaction is achieved by repeating the past, regardless of whether that past was pleasurable or not—and even if it was actually painful. Instead of repeating whatever is found gratifying, in other words, gratification is found in repetition itself—even the repetition of pain. This surprising reversal and predominance of the repetition compulsion over the pleasure principle is precisely the problem Freud wrestled with in *Beyond the Pleasure Principle* (1953, vol. 18), where he introduced the notion of the death instinct.[14] Deleuze and Guattari argue that he was right to question and reverse the presumed relation of repetition to pleasure and that he was right about the "silence" of death—or rather the silencing of death—in modern society, but wrong to subsume them under an "instinct" and project them onto the human psyche *sub specie aeternitatis*.

The implications of Freud's instinctualization of death are several. For one thing, anxiety would on this view be attributed not to the social repression of libido, but to instinct, which itself gives rise to sexual repression instead: social formations would thereby be absolved of any responsibility for repression, as I suggested—and psychoanalysis loses all force as social critique. Perhaps more important, death construed as an instinct necessitates and justifies "civilizing" acts of repression—just the kind of act that results from the Oedipus complex, according to Freud: whereas libido was not necessarily a threat to civilization, and in sublimated forms actually fosters social relations, death is certainly a threat—and so civilization must turn the death instinct against itself via the internalization of castrating paternal authority and the formation of a superego.[15] Freud's death-instinct theory thus ends up justifying the severity of the asceticism inherent in the nuclear family.

And so it is here that schizoanalysis leads psychoanalysis to the point of autocritique and restores its critical force by historicizing it. In modern society, death falls silent and may appear to be an instinct because wealth has been subordinated to value, enjoyment has been subordinated to accumulation, and ends have been subordinated to means by capital: the repetition compulsion takes greater precedence over the pleasure principle because of the aggravation of separation anxiety resulting from the condition of precarious dependence on the capitalist market. Thus, Sadism and Masochism, as disturbances of the repetition compulsion, result from capital's exacerbation of separation anxiety, with Sadistic gratification arising from the pleasure of torture endlessly repeated, and Masochistic gratification arising from a pleasure endlessly deferred, as we have seen.

Lacan and Language

Not surprisingly, given that Guattari trained with Lacan, schizoanalysis is in many ways closer to the Lacanian version of psychoanalysis than to Freud's original version. But it, too, is found to be insufficiently historical. Lacan's famous evacuation of the authority of the psychoanalyst, for example—henceforth understood as occupying the position of a "subject who is supposed to know," but in fact does not (Lacan 1977, 232)—is shown to be a symptom of the evacuation of social authority in a market society based on meaningless axioms rather than codes, as diagnosed in fictions ranging from existentialist novels to *Rollerball*.[16] And the consequences of seeing the market rather than a Symbolic order as the fulcrum of social organization are profound, but discrepant. Like the ancient Greek agora, the market as an immanent multiplicity free from absolute authority is conducive to philosophy (and to Lacanian psychoanalysis as well). It also supports the liberal and existentialist projects of creating meaning for oneself (with the essential proviso that one has the material resources to do so), which at the outer limit of idiosyncratic semiotic free play Deleuze and Guattari call "schizophrenia." Yet as the codes that once ascribed meaning and qualitative value to specified objects succumb to the decoding and strictly quantitative valuation accompanying axiomatization, what Lacan (2006, 431, 439) called the "metonymy of desire" gets detached from the anchor points (2006, 419; *points de capiton*) of socially sanctioned objects—thereby reinforcing the drive to produce and consume more and more, which Norman O. Brown diagnosed as "the meaning of history."[17] Moreover, paternal authority in the segregated nuclear family now floats relatively free, for better or worse, from erstwhile social anchors in the patriarchy, relaying only obedience (with respect to the Father function) and self-denial (vis-à-vis the Mother function) from society at large.

The subordinate processes of recoding, meanwhile, take two basic forms, which Deleuze and Guattari (1983, 225) refer to as "cynicism" and "piety": what is accepted as necessary or unavoidable as opposed to what is considered proper and right; forced compliance versus true belief. In market society, social engineering no longer succeeds in making belief in a central social authority absolute (if it ever did); in its place arise various technologies for securing belief in relative and often conflicting social authorities, ranging from science and religion to nationalism and—believe it or not—internet "influencers." In the same moment, various institutions emerge for enforcing compliance, ranging from schools and workplaces to bureaucracies, police, and prisons, ultimately including the market itself.[18] With the implacable advance of decoding, however, as cynicism and forced compliance prevail over pious beliefs, the search for meaning becomes increasingly desperate, and paranoia becomes rampant, as seen in the growth of various supremacisms.[19]

The most important feature for schizoanalysis of Lacanian psychoanalysis, however, is its substitution of language for the nuclear family as the basis of the Oedipus complex, which gives rise among other things to the language-based concept of schizophrenia central to schizoanalysis.[20] Castration is no longer understood to be the result of paternal authority restricting the child's access to the mother, but of the subject's entry into language and signification, which supposedly separates the now-split subject from both its bodily drives and the objects of those drives, rendering the Real "impossible," in Lacan's idiom. For Deleuze and Guattari, however, the Real is not only not impossible; it is absolutely necessary: without some real connection between bodily needs and the environment, humans simply would not survive. Connection to the object is not lost to signification, as Lacanians would have it, but merely attenuated by filters arising from language and other social representations; in this respect, all objects are partial objects.[21] Schizophrenia scrambles these filters, and schizophrenia according to Deleuze and Guattari therefore entails a less mediated relation to the Real, as illustrated in Roquentin's experience of the chestnut-tree root.[22] Similarly, drives cannot be completely detached from biological "instinct" for if they were, humans as animals that require some degree of regular contact with their environment for sustenance would die. "Water," for example, is not just a differential value determined by its relations with other signifiers: it has meaning (which is not to say that it has "a" meaning), and that meaning is anchored (*point de capiton*) in the necessarily Real relation between our animal form of life and the environment of the planet. Substituting language—a true human universal—for the Victorian nuclear family as the linchpin of castration is certainly an advance over Freud, but if Lacanian idioms remain insufficiently historicized, they risk pathologizing the human condition, which can't be changed—whereas the point of this project is to instead pathologize capitalism, which can and must be changed, if we are to survive the environmental crisis it has brought upon us.

Schizoanalysis historicizes Lacanian psychoanalysis in three principal ways. However traumatic the loss of objects to signification, the trauma is reinforced and accentuated *nachträglich* by the relations of production of capitalism. Because of so-called primitive accumulation and the private ownership of the means of production, the fruits of productive activity belong not to the producers, but to the capitalist—from whom they must be bought back. Objects are therefore not really lost to signification, Deleuze and Guattari insist: they are "*continually taken from them* [the producers]" by the nature of the capitalist market (1983, 27; original emphasis).

> We know very well where lack—and its subjective correlative—come from. Lack (*manque* [the same term in French for both psychological want and economic scarcity]) is created, planned, and organized in and through social production. . . . The deliberate creation of lack as a function of [the capitalist] market economy is the art of a dominant class. This involves deliberately organizing wants and needs (*manque*) amid an abundance of production; making all of desire teeter and fall victim to the great fear of not having one's needs satisfied. (1983, 28)[23]

Wage labor is a kind of theft, whose contractual form nonetheless makes it appear perfectly fair. But most people know—or at least feel strongly—that they are not paid enough to buy back the goods that they have, in the broadest sense, participated in producing—and that those above them are benefiting more than they themselves. Now according to Lacan, the trauma of signification amplifies the repetition compulsion and fosters the metonymy of desire as a vain attempt to regain the lost object (*objet petit-a*) and restore a whole (Imaginary) identity.[24] But according to schizoanalysis, it is the theft of the objects of production that amplifies the repetition compulsion and fosters the metonymy of desire, launching consumers, as we saw in chapter 1, on a vain attempt to establish their identity through imaginative hedonism and endless consumerism—the cornerstone of Masochism.[25] And regardless of how traumatic the entry into signification may seem from a Lacanian perspective, every advertisement actually reinforces the trauma of capitalist production relations, whereby the theft of the fruits of our productive activity compels us to fabricate neurotic, trauma-based consumer identities in compensation. Capital's capture of desire through imaginative hedonism is all the more insidious because of the extent to which it takes place in fantasy even while being denied in reality.[26] Hence the intensity of feelings of *ressentiment* that end up fueling the various forms of supremacism so prevalent in advanced capitalist societies.

Furthermore, the eclipse of the punitive paternal superego in Lacan dovetails with Foucault's (1990) historical debunking of the "repressive hypothesis," according to which the function of the superego was to deny gratification: to the contrary, the superego imperative now is "Enjoy!" (Lacan 1998; Žižek 1999). As capital, in response to crises of overproduction, adds the capture/exploitation of consumptive purchasing power to the capture/exploitation of productive labor power, the social superego imperative is no longer just to deny yourself to produce more for the sake of accumulation, but also to consume more and enjoy yourself—for the sake of accumulation.[27] Of course, you still have to obey the boss at work, and/or obey market forces to become what Foucault called an "entrepreneur of the self" (2004b), so the twin imperatives to obey the Other and enjoy your self split the subject and form the classic, schizophrenogenic double-bind hypothesized by Bateson (1972). Lacan's split subject of signification is thus reinforced and exacerbated *nachträglich* by the ever-growing gulf between production and consumption that propagates borderline conditions, as we have seen. Indeed, Lacan's analysis of what he calls "university discourse" can be read (Zupančič 2006; see also Tomšič 2015) as acknowledging that jouissance as libidinal surplus enjoyment compensating for loss (i.e., theft) gets captured by capital as economic surplus value—thereby updating Marcuse's notion of surplus repression as surplus enjoyment instead, as befits the Protestant consumer ethos of post-Protestant-work-ethic capitalism.[28] But in an uncanny repetition of Freud's recognition that "the death instinct is a product of the capitalist system" in the process of denying it, Lacan acknowledges the historical change undergone by the superego in the process of dismissing historical explanation of it as too much trouble: "Something changed in the master's discourse at a certain point in history. We are not going to break our backs finding out if it was because of Luther, or Calvin, or some unknown traffic of ships around Genoa, or in the Mediterranean Sea, or anywhere else, for the important point is that on a certain day surplus *jouissance* became calculable, could be counted, totalized. This is where what is called the accumulation of capital begins" (Lacan 2007, 177). But if the important point is to change the world rather than interpret it in various ways, historical explanation will have to count for more than psychocentric guesses as to what happened on a certain day in history.

There is, finally, another side to jouissance, which schizoanalysis also historicizes.[29] Jouissance can refer not only to the satisfaction/dissatisfaction of endlessly pursuing substitutes for lost objects, but also to the enjoyment of useless expenditure or waste. Jouissance, Lacan says at one point, "is what serves no purpose [La jouissance, c'est ce qui ne sert à rien]" (1998, 10). For Deleuze and Guattari, however—here (1983, 4) echoing the "general economy" of Georges Bataille—useless expenditure is not merely a matter of personal enjoyment: it is the very foundation and raison-d'être of social organization. No society, Bataille showed in *The Accursed Share* (1998), is actually organized around needs and the production of use values to meet needs—as necessary as such production remains to the survival of the species. For schizoanalysis, similarly, social organization is almost always based on the useless expenditure of excess, which Deleuze and Guattari call "anti-production;" and in a significant departure from orthodox Marxism, productive activity derives its meaning and purpose from such expenditure, rather than the other way around: it is "the activity of anti-production," they insist, "that drives the entire productive system" (1983, 236).[30] Fourth of July fireworks and sports are ready-to-hand examples of the enjoyment gleaned from the useless expenditure of resources and energy; Deleuze and Guattari reference "advertising, civil government, militarism, and imperialism" as other parts of the "gigantic enterprise of anti-production" lying at the heart of capitalism (1983, 235). But for Deleuze and Guattari as well as Bataille, what distinguishes capitalist society from all others is that instead of preventing the accumulation of power, as in the potlatch expenditure rituals of Savagery, or monopolizing the accumulation of power, as in the glorious expenditure of Despotism, capital has captured most forms of antiproduction solely in order to reproduce itself as means of production on an ever-expanding scale. Ends have been subordinated to means, and the accumulation of means has become endless. The joys of useless expenditure, both individual and collective, are sacrificed to the endless accumulation of capital.

The capture of antiproduction for the sake of endless accumulation is not just distinctive of capitalism: it spells the end of civilization as we know it. Capitalism cannot survive without constant growth, and we will not survive with it. Capital's Sadistic relations of production combined with the Masochistic consumerism they require to forestall crises of underconsumption are on course to exhaust and destroy the carrying capacity of the planet. These perversions of the market are the result of what capital does to markets, by subordinating the psychodynamics of the family and signification to the psychodynamics of the market and by axiomatizing factors of production and consumption for the sake of endless private accumulation instead of joyous collective expenditure. Hence the importance of thoroughly historicizing both Freudian and Lacanian psychoanalysis and of understanding the sociodynamics of capitalism as an axiomatic system, the subject of the next chapter.

Chapter Four

The Sociodynamics of the Capitalist Market

Axiomatization

There are according to Deleuze two enemies of difference, two ways of arresting change and obscuring specificity: "the qualitative order of resemblances and the quantitative order of equivalences"; naming and counting (Deleuze 1994, 1). Deleuze and Guattari's analysis of capitalism draws on the difference between these two enemies of difference. The world-historical importance of capitalism is no longer understood to be its continual augmentation of productive force, which looming environmental catastrophe has revealed to be at best a double-edged sword: it is rather its tendency to replace naming with counting as the very basis of social organization, to subordinate the qualitative codes enabling meaning to the quantitative axioms governing market exchange. Instigated by the imperative to accumulate capital, axiomatization too is a double-edged sword, as long it remains yoked to that imperative. The utopian prospect of freeing difference from fixed meaning is clouded by the reality of the capitalist form of axiomatization, which subordinates the collective enjoyment of wealth to the private appropriation of surplus value.

Since market axioms are what is distinctive about capitalist social organization, Deleuze and Guattari analyze the capitalist market as the recording surface of an axiomatic system (Deleuze and Guattari 1983, chapter 3; 1987, plateaus 12 and 13). In mathematics, an axiomatic system is a logically consistent theory all of whose statements can be derived from a set of basic axioms—postulates taken as the point of departure for the derivation of the system, without themselves being derived from any other statements. Crucially, axioms are "real abstractions," a concept derived from Marx's analysis of commodified abstract labor (1983, 270) and developed by Alfred Sohn-Rethel (1978), Moishe Postone (1993), and Jason Moore (2015). As abstract statements, axioms are indifferent to content: a given axiomatic system can give rise to a number of different models when specific meanings are assigned to the abstract terms of the axioms. And that is why axiomatic theory is so important to a critical understanding of the sociodynamics of capitalism: once the private accumulation of surplus value takes precedence over the enjoyment of wealth, the basis of social organization has become abstract and indifferent to content. The fundamental axiom of the capitalist system is the collective production and private appropriation of ever more surplus value through the exploitation of waged producer-consumers, technology, and natural resources. The content of this axiom is immaterial: it doesn't matter what is produced and consumed, or which technologies and natural resources are used—as long as people can be programmed to seek their salvation in private (and often invidious) consumerism rather than shared enjoyment, and surplus value gets appropriated in the process.[1] Correlatively, the basic axiom of capital can be realized in a number of different models, ranging from the erstwhile liberal-democratic capitalisms of the post-war United States and Western Europe to the state capitalisms of the former Soviet Union and Communist China.

Unlike axiomatic systems in most mathematics,[2] which attain absolute consistency by being closed (i.e., comprised of a limited number of axioms and the statements derived from them), the axiomatic system of capital is open and dynamic—and in fact is open because it is dynamic. The system's dynamism stems from the axiomatic imperative to forever accumulate additional quantities of surplus value, and this requires that the system be open to adding and/or subtracting any number of supplemental axioms in the attempt to maintain the system's relative consistency—its consistency, that is, relative to always-changing historical circumstances.[3] Capital is in this respect like any life-form that constantly surveys its environment seeking out sources of nourishment—only in this case, what counts as nourishment is value rather than substance, and the search is guided not by visual, olfactory, or chemical cues but by price differentials as they register on the surface of the world market.

Finally, and now departing from the field of mathematics altogether, capitalist axioms are operational rather than merely stipulative or definitional (as they are in mathematics): they operate by joining together de-coded flows of matter and/or energy in order to produce surplus value (or to reproduce the conditions amenable to the private accumulation of surplus value). Thus, the basic axiom of capital conjoins abstract labor-power with liquid wealth in order to produce surplus value and goods. Liquid wealth is de-coded inasmuch as it is not incarnated in land, private luxury goods, or preexisting means of production, and so is available for investment in cutting-edge means of production that will be competitive on the capitalist market. Labor-power is de-coded in at least two senses: the skills required of labor are determined only after capital has been invested in specific means of production, and more importantly, what ultimately counts for the production of surplus-value is the amount of time spent working rather than the qualities or the results of the work-activity actually performed. As capital expands, supplementary axioms engage and conjoin additional de-coded flows.

Now in order to complete our understanding of the capitalist market as the recording surface of an open and dynamic axiomatic system and of axiomatization as a dynamic operation, two additional distinctions are required: we need to distinguish between intensive and extended multiplicities, and between non-metric (intensive) quantities and metric quantities.[4] And in light of our interest in the dynamics of axiomatization, the issue is not merely the static difference between non-metric quantities such as distance or depth and metric quantities such as length, but more importantly the conversion of non-metric quantities into metric or metricized quantities—since such conversion is required and performed by the process of axiomatization. Fortunately, Bertrand Russell treats both issues with consummate clarity in his *Principles of Mathematics* (1938).[5]

The difference between distance and length is sometimes subtle, but of the utmost importance. On a color wheel, for example, we can say that red is at a greater distance from yellow than orange is, but that distance is nonmetric: it cannot be measured; it is not a length. In much the same vein, standing on a narrow ledge 100 meters high is not 20 times scarier than standing on one 5 meters high: it may well be scarier, much scarier, but the difference is not susceptible to linear measurement. Having distinguished categorically between distance and length, Russell goes on to specify how the former can be converted into the latter, by the application of two axioms: the axiom of continuity (a.k.a. Archimedes' axiom) and the axiom of linearity, which I will refer to as the axioms of "comparability" and "homogeneity," respectively.[6] The first stipulates that, given two terms, one will be larger than the other (more precisely, that a finite multiple of one will be larger than the other, even though the multiple may be unknown); the second stipulates that a given quantity can be divided into equal (homogeneous) parts. Thus, once color terms are converted into wavelengths of light, we can say that (some shade of) "red" (with a wavelength of 700 nanometers) is twice as far from "yellow" (600 nanometers) as "orange" (650 nanometers) is, or that "cyan" (500) is exactly as far from "blue" (450) as it is from "green" (550). An intensive difference between colors has been converted into a metricized difference between wavelengths. And this difference between intensive and metric is not just a matter of perception, of the distinction between what have been called "primary" ("objective") and "secondary" ("subjective") qualities: it can be a real distinction. Temperature, for example, is both intensive and objective: 10° is not twice as hot as 5°, and the 10° difference between water temperatures of −5°C and +5°C is completely distinct from the 10°difference between +5°C and +15°C; solid ≠ liquid; ice ≠ water; 10° ≠ 10°.

Like temperature, depth, and distance, the capitalist market, too, can be understood as an intensive multiplicity, a kind of virtual space or surface that registers commercial transactions and economic value in terms of prices. Thus, the difference between paying $5 and paying $10 for one pair of shoes is completely distinct from the difference between paying $295 and paying $300 for a different pair of shoes: $5 ≠ $5. In a similar vein, no one paying $300 for a single pair of shoes is likely to buy twenty pairs of shoes costing $15 each: $300 ≠ $300. And yet, on the recording surface of the market, one pair of $300 shoes is evidently the same as twenty pairs of $15 shoes: $300 = $300. So, from the perspective of investment capital, in sharp contrast with that of producer-consumers, $300 might well equal $300, whether invested in high-fashion stilettos or cheap sneakers.[7] It begins to look as though the market surface under capitalism is asymmetrical and has two sides, one facing producer consumers, the other facing investment capital, only one of which answers to the axiom of homogeneity whereby a dollar always and everywhere equals precisely one dollar.[8]

This appearance of equality or equal exchange on the market surface is of paramount importance—the market simply could not function without it—and yet it is at the same time extremely misleading. For, appearances notwithstanding, capital investors are buyers, too, in their own way—and over time, given the vagaries of supply and demand, those twenty pairs of $15 sneakers might turn out to be worth more than a single pair of stilettos that has fallen out of fashion (or conversely: a capital-investor might buy twenty pairs of sneakers at $15/pair but only be able to sell ten pairs at that price, meaning that the originally purchased pairs actually turned out to be worth only $150). That is to say, if the market presents an intensive surface to producer-consumers for reasons of subjective evaluation, the surface it presents to investment capital is equally intensive, but for different reasons: the factors of time, contingency, and risk. Many economists—from Frank Wright, John Maynard Keynes, and Hyman Minsky to Nassim Taleb and Elie Ayache more recently—have insisted on the inherent unpredictability of investment outcomes and the resulting impossibility of grounding investment decisions on any practicable calculation whatsoever. And yet the point of departure for such decisions—the only possible existing point of departure—is the state of the market at a given time: a completely if only punctually metricized surface where homogeneous exchange value reigns and, if only for a moment, a dollar everywhere equals precisely one dollar.

This account of the capitalist market surface as two-sided and asymmetrical enables us to identify four features that distinguish capitalist markets from markets in general or in the abstract. The first such feature is production for the market. Indeed, Deleuze and Guattari propose that it is production for the market that makes capitalism an axiomatic system to begin with (1987, 436). Markets, of course, have existed in various forms for millennia; but production for the market is distinctive of capitalism in both its stages or versions: in so-called mercantile capitalism as well as in capitalism properly so-called (i.e., "industrial" and "postindustrial" capitalism). The asymmetry of the specifically capitalist market reflects the fact that whereas producer consumers sell in order to buy, capital investors buy in order to sell: producer consumers sell their labor power in order to buy goods to consume; capital investors buy factors of production in order to produce and then sell goods and thereby accumulate surplus value.[9]

The second feature enables us to further distinguish mercantile capitalism from capitalism proper and revolves around the distinction between what Deleuze and Guattari call the "surplus-value of code" characteristic of precapitalist societies and the "surplus-value of flow" characteristic of capitalist society.[10] Well before capitalism emerged, money-mediated market exchange involved translating the actual, substantial, and qualitative value of products brought to market into the virtual, abstract, and quantified value incarnated in money, in order to eventually convert virtual value back into substantial value through the purchase of different products, the ones taken from the market to be consumed. The price as incarnation of virtual value here represents a local and punctual consensus about the value of exchanged products in a given context at a given time. The basic arrangement remains the same even under what is called "mercantile capitalism," where a capital investor (the "middle man") starts with money rather than a product and intervenes between the initial production and the final consumption (both of which are independent of the market and of no concern to the merchant) in order to turn a profit by "buying low and selling high"—that is, by buying already produced, actual products for price M at location or time 1 and selling them for M + Δ or M' at location or time 2. Mercantile capital produces a surplus value of code, depending as it does on differences in qualitative evaluation between two distinct locations or times, just as direct money-mediated exchange in the first case depends on a consensus evaluation. Crucially, neither of these markets forms a system.

Properly capitalist markets, by contrast, produce a surplus value of flow and form a complete system because of the third distinctive feature of capitalism: the commodification of labor power and the apparent metricization (qualitative homogenization and quantitative determination) of exchange value by abstract labor time. Exchanging labor power as a commodity for money strips all kinds of works of their qualitative specificity inasmuch as they are thereby rendered equivalent in value to one another (and to all other commodities). And it makes not the nature or quality of the work but an abstract quantity—homogeneous labor time—the common measure of exchange value throughout a single system: the world market. It is the apparent metricization of value by labor power that makes it possible to speak of "the" market in the singular: a single recording surface that now spans the entire globe. Of course, "the" market is in fact composed of a patchwork of submarkets: the housing market, the stock market, national and regional markets, the job market, the derivatives market, emerging markets, the subprime market, and so forth. But metricization establishes the axiomatic comparability of value across any and all of these submarkets—and enables investment decisions to be made on this basis.[11] The market thus presents capital with an apparently homogeneous intensive surface—a surface that is real but not actual—across which it will search for investment opportunities calculated—or rather: hopefully projected—to turn a profit.

Here again, it is essential to recognize that the appearance of homogeneity is misleading, even if it is absolutely necessary for the capitalist market to function. The axiomatic imperative of capital, as I have said, is to produce surplus value, not wealth (or value itself). And all the production of surplus value requires is for there to be a positive difference between the flow of value V paid to workers (the cost of reproducing their labor power, called "variable capital") to produce goods and the flow of value V + Δ realized from the sale of those goods, a difference pocketed and accumulated by the capitalist. To this "human surplus value of variable capital," Deleuze and

Guattari add the "machinic surplus value of constant capital" (1983, 237) based on the axioms of science and technology introduced into production processes to make them more efficient. More recently, Jason Moore (2015) has added the surplus value of what he calls "cheap nature" to the capitalist exchange system as a key factor (along with unpaid human work) in reducing reproduction costs to enable the accumulation of surplus value. Furthermore, Anna Tsing (2015) has shown how the world market enables capital to profit from commercial transactions that don't involve abstract labor time at all. In this differential understanding of surplus value, in other words, it is the actual comparability of value that ultimately matters, more than its supposed homogeneity. It is circulation on the market, then, that endows money with the appearance of a metric quantity and the function of homogenizing value across the entire surface of the market.[12]

And not only is value universally commutable in a system metricized by the market in this way, but capital can therefore circulate throughout it as well, taking on different forms without ever ceasing to be capital: the liquid/virtual wealth of an investment bank balance is different from the constant capital invested in actual means of production, and from the variable capital expended on the purchase of labor power, and from the capital incarnated in goods waiting to be sold—yet in all these different forms it remains capital: capital = capital. Production no longer takes place prior to and independent of exchange, as in mercantile capitalism but is planned, organized, and undertaken by the capitalists themselves; and for the capitalist market, consumption itself merely serves to reproduce labor power and return capital to owners for reinvestment (a.k.a. the "realization" of surplus value in liquid form through the sale of commodities): it is therefore no longer independent of the system either. The Δ of the surplus value of flow no longer arises from context-dependent differences of qualitative evaluation, as in mercantile capitalism, but from the flow of value through the system itself. The commodification of labor power provides the homogeneous measure that endows the intensive recording surface of the capitalist market with the appearance of a metric multiplicity. It is (arguably) only in the capitalist system, or perhaps more precisely on the capitalist market, that time = money.

The fourth and final distinctive feature of capitalist markets is, of course, capital itself—which as we have seen changes form as it circulates throughout the capitalist system, without ever ceasing to be capital. But that begs the question of where capital comes from in the first place. Deleuze and Guattari provide one kind of answer in their genealogy of modes of production in chapter 3 of *Anti-Oedipus*: the infinite debt owed to the Despot in the "barbaric" mode of production becomes an infinite debt owed to capital in the "civilized" (capitalist) mode of production (Deleuze and Guattari 1983; Holland 1999, 58–59, 90–91). But a more concrete, historical account of the transfer of the infinite debt from Despot to capital better suits our purpose here, for which the crucial turning point is 1694: the year of the founding of the national Bank of England, on which practically all subsequent national central banks (including the US Federal Reserve Bank) are modeled (Di Muzio and Robbins, 2016). Crucially, instead of being transferred to the modern State itself, the infinite debt gets transferred to a central bank, marking the subordination of what had been a transcendent, Despotic state to the interests of private capital, and especially finance capital (Marx and Engels 1975, vol. 3; Deleuze and Guattari 1983, especially chapter 3). Instead of creating money on its own account, the English government licensed a private bank to do so, thereby enabling the State to prosecute wars to a far greater extent than under preceding money-lending arrangements, but also thereby guaranteeing owners of private capital a return on their loans through the appropriation of a significant share of the government's tax revenue. (The recurrent congressional battles over raising the US debt ceiling is evidence that 1694 marks an important event that still haunts us.) Henceforth, the subordinate functions of the state will include limiting the amount of so-called "fictitious" capital that banks are permitted to create out of thin air to a percentage of the "real" capital already on deposit (referred to as a "reserve ratio") and even more important, controlling the money supply.[13] To suit the interest of finance capital, money can neither be so plentiful as to preclude banks from charging interest for loaning it out nor so tight as to choke off the production and consumption undertaken on the underside of the market in order to generate the funds necessary to pay the loans back.[14] The domination of modern capitalist markets by finance capital has at least three significant consequences.

The first and perhaps most important consequence is that the capitalist market surface is not a tabula rasa or an even playing field, as it were: it has a slope; it is slanted by the pressure always to accumulate more capital, both to prevail over rival capitalists and, increasingly and more significantly, to pay back with interest the funds borrowed to make investments in the first place since banks always loan principal only, never the money to pay the interest. (One result is the absolute requirement that the capitalist economy continue to grow—with the disastrous environmental consequences of which we are only now becoming cognizant.) Second, the investment decisions determining the distribution of finance capital across the market surface are not qualitative or evaluative but purely ordinal or differential: they are not intrinsically concerned with what to produce, or where, or for whom; all that matters is successfully fighting the slope so as to avoid sliding off the market surface altogether. The basic axiomatic imperative is therefore not just "buy low; sell high" (an axiom of unequal exchange that applies equally to mercantile capitalism), but rather what we might call the "axiom of differential accumulation," which is both abstract (indifferent to content, to what is produced/consumed[15]) and purely differential (strictly relative to the returns of other capitalists and the prevailing interest rates): every capitalist must earn more than the average return, or eventually get acquired or go bankrupt.[16]

Finally, what I have called the "asymmetry" and "slope" of the capitalist market are a matter not just of structure, but of force: production and consumption are undertaken on the underside of the market principally in order to generate the funds necessary to pay back the loans issued on the top side. Unlike precapitalist markets, in other words, the primary (axiomatic) function of the capitalist market is not the production, exchange, or consumption of goods, but the registration of obligations and the generation of means to repay the infinite debt.[17] Money, as we have seen, has always been a repository of virtual value, but the power of finance capital is not merely money's ability to appropriate (to actualize as mine) an object that was already produced: it is the ability to actualize production itself. What is crucial is not just that, unlike spiders with their webs, humans produce goods in the imagination before producing them in actual reality; it is that, under capitalism, decisions as to if and what to produce, and as to when and how and where, are all made in the virtual realm, on the intensive surface of the market, before a single dollar is actually invested, before the first factory actually gets built, and before the first workers actually get hired; only after that do the goods in all their posthoc determinacy actually get produced for eventual sale and use, in the hope of turning a profit on the initial investment. That is to say, the vast and complex network of actual producers and consumers comprising the global capitalist economy comes into being as an *extended multiplicity* only after and as a consequence of calculations or projections based on prices inscribed on the recording surface of the market as an *intensive multiplicity*.

A multiplicity can be defined as a formation made up of contingent articulations among heterogeneous elements, and a multiplicity such as the world market has two aspects: intensive and extended.[18] Among the elements comprising the extended multiplicity of the world market are the locations of natural resources distributed across the globe, which are themselves located at variable distances from the production facilities that can process them. Those distances are converted to metric lengths (i.e., are axiomatized), and those metric distances are then translated into transportation costs, which get factored into the cost of production. In addition to natural-resource and factory locations, there are the locations of wholesale distribution hubs and retail outlets, with the distances among those also converted into lengths and transportation costs and then factored into distribution costs. The extended multiplicity of the world market also includes the global distribution of producers and consumers relative to production facilities and retail outlets, along with the locations and reach of purveyors of production skills, consumer tastes, and production technologies (schools, advertising, research universities). Considered as an extended multiplicity, then, the world market consists of a vast network of heterogeneous resource, production, and consumption nodes knit together by an open and constantly changing set of contingent articulations. And given the capitalist imperative of perpetual accumulation, the world market is constantly expanding as well as changing, which results in the continual development of the division of labor and a corresponding division of leisure. Constant expansion means the increasing differentiation and specialization of job skills and work activities, as well as the increasing differentiation and specialization of consumer tastes and leisure activities.

Crucially, the world market must be understood not just as an extended multiplicity, but also as an intensive multiplicity, in which capacity it serves, as we have suggested, as the recording surface for capitalist axiomatization. Despite the appearance of metric homogeneity, this recording surface is nonmetric. Needless to say, this intensive aspect of the market is in no way independent of the extended market: both investment and purchasing decisions made on the basis of prices registered on the intensive recording surface produce actual changes in the extended market, and such changes will in turn affect pricing on the recording surface. But that does not mean that investment and purchasing decisions have an equal impact on the market: the decisions of producer consumers are largely constrained by the decisions of investment capital, regarding both the jobs and the goods that are and are not made available to them. The function of money as an instrument of debt subsumes its function as an instrument of exchange (Graeber 2011). Onto the horizontal set of differential relations comprising the divisions of labor and leisure on the world market, then, finance capital superimposes a vertical binary power hierarchy whereby production and consumption are required to answer to the imperative of endless accumulation.

Like any stratum, the world market is doubly articulated, to adapt the analytic Deleuze and Guattari borrowed from Hjelmslevian linguistics.[19] Strata articulate a component of content and a component of expression, each including both form and substance. The substance of content of the world market is the network of resources, factories, outlets, and populations; its form of content is an extended multiplicity: a contingent and constantly changing assemblage of people, places, and things existing in geographical space. The substance of expression of the world market is money (as intensive repository of virtual value), and its form of expression is bifurcated, depending on the kind of relation to the market: as a source of livelihood and identity, the form of expression is Masochism; as a source of surplus value, the form of expression is Sadism.

Now to express the political force of this asymmetry, using protolinguistic terms, Deleuze and Guattari distinguish between investment capital as the subject of enunciation and the extended economy as subject of statements—that is, subject to the operative investment statements made by capital.[20] Deleuze and Guattari offer off-shore outsourcing as an illustration. Faced with declining profits at home and lured by the prospect of greater returns from abroad, a transnational corporation as subject of enunciation might move production overseas—that is to say, add an axiom on the intensive recording surface of the market that changes the location of production facilities as subject of the statement on the extended market. Later, the corporation might reverse course and repatriate those facilities—canceling the overseas axiom (Deleuze and Guattari 1987, 463–64). This investment decision could be based simply on insufficient profits from the overseas facility, or it could stem from tax breaks offered by legislators responding to pressure from citizens to create more jobs at home. In both cases, the investment decision involves a primary or capital axiom based solely on comparing projected returns. But in the second case, it also involves the legislature as subject of enunciation issuing a secondary or state axiom that alters capital's calculus in favor of creating local jobs as subject of the statement. Since states are no longer sovereign entities, as they were under Despotism, but merely serve as "models of realization" (1987, 454; 1994, 106) for the capitalist axiomatic, capital axioms take precedence over state axioms; yet the state is itself a battleground of competing interests, where the public good can sometimes prevail over the private interest of capital. This second case is indeed an example of the "struggle on the level of the axioms" that Deleuze and Guattari insist (1987, 463, 470–71) is so important, although it must be said that on the whole, the ensemble of state axioms has so far always heavily favored capital.

The power asymmetry between capital and the extended market is also couched by Deleuze and Guattari in more recognizably economic terms. Adapting the analyses of Suzanne de Brunhoff (1971), they distinguish between two circuits of money: one of investment capital circulating from banks to productive enterprises and back (with interest), the other of what we could call "remuneration capital" circulating from employers to producer consumers as wages and back (when consumers buy back from capitalists the products they have produced for them).[21] And in terms adapted from anthropology, they distinguish between rigid and supple segmentation: the former referring to the overcoding of money via the double pincer of abstract labor and state-regulated currency; the latter characterizing the domain of goods actually produced, exchanged, and consumed (Deleuze and Guattari 1987, plateau 9). To this last pair of anthropological terms, however, Deleuze and Guattari add a third term (drawn from a completely different discipline): *quantum flows*. The feature they are borrowing from quantum physics is the undecidability or indeterminacy of the state of some particles (and Schrödinger's cat) before they are observed or measured. The point they are emphasizing is that above and below both rigid and supple segmentation are flows that escape segmentation altogether.

The addition of this third term presents a more complete diagram of the capitalist market, with supple segmentation serving as a battleground of struggle between rigid segmentarity and quantum flows that cannot be captured in their entirety. In much the same way that the Despot issued currency to capture flows of surplus goods converted into tribute payments, capital issues credit money in order to capture flows of surplus value. But before being denominated in an actual loan to be invested in factors of production, credit money takes the intensive form of a quantum flow of yet-to-be-measured value, of pure creative potential—which Deleuze and Guattari (1987, 492) refer to as "smooth capital." Smooth capital is distinguished from the "striated capital" that gets denominated and invested in the production of surplus value, based on correlated segmentations of labor time, wage payments, production output, commodity prices, and other factors of production and consumption (scientific knowledges, technologies, fads, taste, etc.): "Not only does each line have its segments, but the segments of one line correspond to those of another; for example, the wage regime establishes a correspondence between monetary segments, production segments, and consumable-goods segments" (1987, 212). On the capitalist market, rigid segmentarity appears in the actions of state-sanctioned central banks, which issue and validate currency; supple segmentation characterizes the aggregate of exchanges actually transacted via the medium of money; and supple segmentation in turn depends on quantum flows of desire for enjoyment in abundance, only some of which get captured and converted into commercial transactions. On both sides of the two-sided capitalist market, then, intensive quantum flows—of abstract value on the top side, and of desire on the underside—fuel the processes of rigid and supple segmentation comprising the capitalist economy.

So, given that capitalism as a complete system consists of "*a general axiomatic of decoded flows*," we know perfectly well what two of those flows are: "capitalism forms when the flow of unqualified [indeterminate] wealth encounters the flow of unqualified [indeterminate] labor and conjugates with it" (1987, 453; emphasis in original). But to say that the capitalist axiomatic forms a *complete* system does not mean that it is a *closed* system. On the contrary, as Deleuze and Guattari insist (no doubt drawing on Lautman's [1938] account of the dynamics of axiomatic structuralism in mathematics), axioms get added to and subtracted from the capitalist axiomatic for a host of reasons, as long as they reinforce the continuing conjugation of liquid wealth and commodified labor on which capital principally depends: "A single axiomatic seems capable of encompassing polymorphic models" (1987, 455).[22] We arrive, then, at a picture of the worldwide market as providing a smooth space, an intensive pricing surface, for capital to explore in search of flows of matter and energy to axiomatize in order to produce and accumulate surplus value and pay down the infinite debt.

Historically, one of the main reasons for adding axioms has been legal limitations placed on the length of the working day, so to the extraction of absolute surplus-value by forcing workers to work more hours than required to pay their wages is added the extraction of relative surplus-value by making the hours they are permitted to work more productive. This entails the transformation of work through the introduction of scientific technology. Although not expressed directly in terms of price, scientific technology metricizes intensive flows of matter and energy in its own way, thereby making them susceptible to subsequent axiomatization as quantifiable factors of production on the market where their cost gets priced. Even with prescientific, craft production technologies, work has always involved attending to intensive properties of matter/energy in order to counteractualize one actual factor of production (a piece of wood, say) by transforming it into an actual finished product (a salad bowl or sculpture). But prior to the development of capitalist production, this "attending to the intensive properties" of factors of production meant mobilizing capacities, skills, and know-how developed immanently in context over time and instilled in laborers through apprenticeships. With the advent of capitalism, two crucial changes occur. First of all, laborers are uprooted from their local context and obliged to work on means of production that are provided by capital from on high and for which they have to be trained anew: the labor power taken out of context has been decoded, and then recoded depending on the specifics of the means of production furnished by capital—specifics which themselves emerge only after the operative investment statements to invest liquid wealth in this or that productive enterprise have been made. Second, the know-how once embodied in workers is extracted from the workplace and developed in the laboratory into the abstract and supposedly context-free knowledge of royal science, ready to be reintroduced as technology into the production process as another factor of production.[23] (As we saw in chapter 1, it was Sir Francis Bacon who initiated this process in England, proposing to send agents of the Royal Academy to extract practical knowhow from workshops throughout England in order to transform it into state-sanctioned, abstract scientific knowledge.[24]) With conception increasingly segregated from and elevated above execution for these reasons (with intellectual labor elevated above manual labor), one result is that workers get deprived of agency at the workplace (reaching its nadir, perhaps, in the Taylorist assembly line)—which they vainly attempt to reclaim as consumers in the dynamic I have identified as Masochism. Another result is that the distribution of state-sanctioned knowledge segments among the population gets correlated with the distribution of wage segments, with higher rates of remuneration generally corresponding with access to greater amounts and/ or more specialized segments of scientific knowledge (Protevi 2013, 107–8).

For our purposes, however, the most important result of the separation of conception from execution was the development of a state form of thought—revolving around what Deleuze and Guattari call the "numbered number" (1987, 390–91)—that metricizes all of matter and energy by translating "secondary qualities" (such as color perception) into "primary qualities" (e.g., wavelengths of light) expressed in strictly mathematical terms.[25] Compared to the form of thought characteristic of "Savagery," this state form of thought mobilizes precisely the comparability and homogenization on which capitalist axiomatization will depend: "Instead of traits of expression that follow a machinic phylum and wed it in a distribution of singularities [as in Savage thought], the State constitutes a form of expression that subjugates the phylum: the phylum or matter is no longer anything more than an equalized, homogenized, compared content, while expression becomes a form of resonance or appropriation" (1987, 444–45).[26] Compared to the imperial state, the modern (capitalist) state applies the metrics of the numbered number and context-free royal science to all of matter, no longer only to human populations:

> Arithmetic, the number, has always had a decisive role in the State apparatus: this is so even as early as the imperial bureaucracy, with the three conjoined operations of the census, taxation, and election. It is even truer of modern forms of the State. . . . [Here] this arithmetic element of the State found its specific power in the treatment of all kinds of matter: primary matters (raw materials), the secondary matter of wrought objects, or the ultimate matter constituted by the human population. Thus the number has always served to gain mastery over matter, to control its variations and movements. (1987, 389)

The applied branch of royal science thus ends up mapping intensive properties of matter and energy so that knowledge of them can be fed into the production process to make it more efficient and generate more relative surplus value.[27] So not just flows of matter and energy, but flows of technology itself get commodified and axiomatized as knowledge factors in investment decisions made on the market surface, whether a capitalist enterprise hires and pays its own scientists to produce such knowledge, pays licensing fees to use knowledge produced by others, or buys machinery with the knowledge, so to speak, already built in.[28]

Turning to the last of the four basic flows comprising the capitalist axiomatic, it must be said that Deleuze and Guattari's discussion of human populations in terms of axiomatization reintroduces a certain amount of terminological confusion in relation to set theory proper. But the core of their analysis is well worth retrieving or reconstructing by paying careful attention to which features of a given mathematical concept are to be retained and which ignored. We have seen, for example, that segments of state-sanctioned productive knowledge get correlated with wage segments—and this can be construed as the effect of an axiomatic national education system that, in principle, offers equal opportunity to all members of its student population, even if the effects of other axioms often prevent some such opportunities from being realized or even offered. Similarly, segments of consumer taste get correlated with segments of purchasing power as an effect of axioms conducted by advertising addressed to anyone, even if these axioms tend to emerge and disappear more rapidly than those of the education system. Finally, one key feature of the modern state is the tenet of equality before the law: in principle, everyone has the same standing and receives equal treatment in the legal system—although here again, effects of other axioms often prevent realization of the principle.[29]

What these examples have in common is the axiom of homogeneity: human populations are manageable through their treatment as what Deleuze and Guattari call "denumerable sets"—which parallels the metricization of nonhuman matter through primary qualities. Denumerable sets are important for two reasons. First, it is only as an undifferentiated (decoded) mass of homogeneous "equals" that humans can be counted and human populations quantified so that they can be axiomatized since "the axiomatic manipulates only denumerable sets" (1987, 470).[30] Even more important, denumerable sets will be contrasted with nondenumerable sets—a contrast that lies at the heart of Deleuze and Guattari's political philosophy and aligns term-for-term with the distinction between major and minor: "What defines a minority, then, is not the number but the relations internal to the number. A minority can be numerous, or even infinite; so can a majority. What distinguishes them is that in the case of a majority the relation internal to the number constitutes a set that may be finite or infinite, but is always denumerable, whereas the minority is defined as a non-denumerable set, however many elements it may have" (1987, 470). But it is here, as Jon Roffe has shown (2016), that the terminological confusion arises, for nondenumerable sets in set theory proper are such only because of their size ("the (uncountable) continuum"), with nondenumerable sets always being larger than denumerable sets (even when both are infinite).[31] For Deleuze and Guattari, however, what defines a minor nondenumerable set is not size but what we might call a particular mode-of-belonging[32]—which is completely irrelevant to denumerable sets: "What characterizes the non-denumerable is neither the set nor its elements; rather, it is the connection, the 'and' produced between elements, between sets, and which belongs to neither, which eludes them and constitutes a line of flight. The axiomatic manipulates only denumerable sets, even infinite ones, whereas the minorities constitute 'fuzzy,' non-denumerable, nonaxiomizable sets, in short, 'masses,' multiplicities of escape and flux" (1987, 470). Members of a denumerable set are homogeneous in that they belong to the set by answering to a common rule or axiom; members of nondenumerable sets are heterogeneous and belong to them "existentially," so to speak, strictly as a matter of fact, without answering to any rules whatsoever. The axiomatization of human populations thus involves the conversion of nondenumerable into denumerable sets—for as Deleuze and Guattari stipulate, the axiomatic always and only manipulates denumerable sets. But the stipulation comes with a crucial proviso: the conversion can never be complete, always entails quantum flows that escape, always leaves, or indeed generates "multiplicities of escape and flux" (1987, 470).

And so we arrive at the political implications of Deleuze and Guattari's theory of capitalist axiomatics, posed as a Problem (or a challenge): under what circumstances will the force of minor, nondenumerable multiplicities be greater than the power of denumerable multiplicities—will the connections of flows producing minor multiplicities be stronger than the conjugation of flows that comprise the capitalist axiomatic? Under propitious circumstances, according to this view, the connection of flows boosts their intensity and produces a result that is greater than the sum of the parts and can even become revolutionary; the conjugation of flows, by contrast, reduces their potential, "performs a general reterritorialization, and brings the flows under the dominance of a single flow capable of overcoding them" (1987, 220). As Deleuze and Guattari put it:

> At the same time as capitalism is effectuated in the denumerable sets serving as its models, it necessarily constitutes nondenumerable sets that cut across and disrupt those models. It does not effect the "conjugation" of the deterritorialized and decoded flows without those flows forging farther ahead; without their escaping both the axiomatic that conjugates them and the models that reterritorialize them; without their tending to enter into "connections" that delineate a new Land; without their constituting a war machine whose aim is . . . revolutionary movement (the connection of flows, the composition of non-denumerable aggregates, the becoming-minoritarian of everybody/everything). (1987, 472–73; emphasis in original)[33]

In a word, minor politics becomes revolutionary when it mobilizes multiplicities of connections in opposition to the conjugations of the axiomatic, with the ultimate aim of "smashing capitalism [and] redefining socialism" (1987, 472). This is the positive or utopian tendency of the capitalist axiomatic and of the extended divisions of labor and leisure to which it gives rise:

to perpetually generate more numerous and potentially more potent minor connections and nondenumerable aggregates than it can possibly recapture for the sake of surplus value.

But there is no guarantee that minor connections will prove stronger than the major conjugations of the axiomatic, even if they are more numerous—which is one reason the political implications of capitalist axiomatization are posed as a Problem by Deleuze and Guattari. For one of the most important tenets of schizoanalysis, based on reconsidering Freud and even Marx from the perspective of Nietzsche, is that desire always invests a greater degree of development of force or energy (1983, 345)[34]—actualized under capitalism in the ever-greater ensemble of capacities generated by the extended divisions of labor and leisure of the world market. To be sure, we consciously construct ends and means in accordance with what we believe to be our rational and/or objective interests, but these aims and objectives are in fact based on "a disinterested love of the social machine, of the form of power, and of the degree of development in and for themselves" (1983, 346). Key here is that, although capital irresistibly attracts libidinal investment because of its always-intensifying development of productive force, it generates two distinct forms of power, through axiomatic conjugation and nondenumerable connections: major and minor, or power over and power with.[35] In the terminology of *Anti-Oedipus* adapted from psychiatry, they were referred to as paranoia and schizophrenia; in the object-relations terminology deployed in chapter 2, they generate the basins of attraction for inhabitants of market society I called "borderline supremacism" and "polymorphous narcissism." And equally important: capitalism as an open axiomatic system depends absolutely on the force of minor connections for its dynamism and hence its very survival. It operates, that is, as an apparatus of capture, relentlessly attempting to axiomatize decoded flows and commodify innovations in production and consumption alike in pursuit of the endless accumulation of surplus value. Given the struggle between the two opposed forms of power characterizing the capitalist axiomatic, three outcomes are foreseeable.

Although Deleuze and Guattari consider the minor "connection of flows, the composition of non-denumerable aggregates, [and] the becoming-minoritarian of everybody/everything" (1987, 473) to be the primary and potentially revolutionary tendency of capital's historical development—it is what makes history universal, in the terms of *Anti-Oedipus*—this does not diminish the significance of struggles that take place within the axiomatic, over the nature of the axioms themselves. On the contrary, they explicitly recognize the importance of a whole range of political movements not directly tied to anticapitalist politics, and even go so far as to assert that the "molecular escapes and movements [of minor politics] would be nothing if they did not return to the molar [or major] organizations to reshuffle their segments, their binary distributions of sexes, classes, and parties" (1987, 216–17). To propose minority as a "universal figure" and the "becoming-everything of everyone (devenir tout le monde)," they insist, "is not to say that the struggle on the level of the axioms is without importance; on the contrary, it is determining (at the most diverse levels: women's struggle for the vote, for abortion, for jobs; the struggle of the regions for autonomy; the struggle of the Third World; the struggle of the oppressed masses and minorities in the East or West)" (1987, 470–71). This focus on reforming axioms within the capitalist axiomatic does not, however, entail establishing some ideal model of democracy or universal list of human rights by which to judge contemporary societies, but rather identifying and supporting tendencies already at work in those societies that might make them more democratic and extend concepts of human rights in new directions. Thus in the "Geophilosophy" section of *What Is Philosophy?*, they repeatedly insist that "there is no universal democratic State" (Deleuze and Guattari 1994, 102 and 106) and highlight instead a process of "becoming-democratic" (1994, 113) that would involve, among other things, the extension of suffrage, the realignment of preexisting public institutions on new goals and the invention of new rights: "When one turns to the justice system . . . it's not a question of applying 'the rights of man' but rather of inventing new forms of jurisprudence" (Deleuze and Parnet 2011, "G as in gauche"). For jurisprudence is the arena in which the pressure of minor social movements can reshape the axioms of the legal system.

As important as bringing the pressure of minor political movements to bear on existing axioms may be, however, it has several problems. Capitalist axioms can simply be revoked by capital at any time, as the rapid elimination in the United States of the axioms of Fordism at the turn of the century vividly illustrates; state axioms, conversely, may tie populations to an acquired status that fails to keep pace with new developments in social life (as restricting marriage to heterosexual couples did, for example). Most important: in both cases, relying on axioms effectively grants to capital and the state organizational control over more and more areas of social life. Ultimately, as important a "tactic" as struggling over axioms may be, Deleuze and Guattari insist that "the struggle around axioms is *most important* when it manifests, itself opens, the gap between two types of propositions, [minor] propositions of flow and [major] propositions of axioms" (1987, 471; emphasis added). For it is the former that are able to escape and challenge the capitalist axiomatic.[36]

This preference for minor propositions of flow over major propositions of axioms is one reason why Deleuze and Guattari claim, in a more revolutionary vein, that "the power of minority . . . finds its figure or universal consciousness in the proletariat": for the proletariat pursues revolution not to improve its position within capitalism but to abolish itself as (variable) capital by eliminating the axioms of capital altogether (1987, 472).[37] But simply abolishing the capitalist axiomatic would mean relinquishing its positive tendencies, which are considerable. It would mean eliminating the difference engine that gives rise to myriad nondenumerable sets and connections and that decodes flows to free us from instinctual, traditional, habitual, and neurotic determinations; it would curtail the expansion of capacities generated by the extended divisions of labor and leisure of the world market. Perhaps most significantly, it would risk reverting to social relations based on more immediately interpersonal and political forms of domination and subordination. For one advantage of market-based social relations, as Marx put it, is that "the power that each individual exercises over the activity of others or over social wealth exists in him as the owner of exchange values, of money. He carries his social power . . . in his pocket . . . in the form of a thing. *Take away this social power from the thing, and you must give it to persons to exercise over persons*" (Marx and Engels 1975, vol. 28, 94–95; emphasis added). Eliminating axiomatization altogether, in other words, would sacrifice the horizontal power with fostered by market-mediated social relations to the vertical power over of unmitigated political domination.[38] Here again, however, it is of the utmost importance to determine the extent to which the positive tendencies of capitalist axiomatization are attributable to the market itself rather than to capital, and thereby to distinguish clearly between capitalist and postcapitalist markets.

For the third possible outcome of the struggle between the axiomatic conjugations of capital and the potentially revolutionary connections they generate is the creation of what Deleuze and Guattari refer to at one point as a "new axiomatic." Ultimately, they suggest, "the power [of minority connections] is not measured by their capacity to enter and make themselves felt within the majority system . . . but [by their capacity] to bring to bear the force of the non-denumerable sets . . . against the denumerable sets . . . even if they imply new axioms *or, most importantly, a new axiomatic*" (1987, 471; translation modified, emphasis added). Although they themselves say nothing more about it, what is so important about a new, postcapitalist axiomatic can be outlined *a contrario* from their analysis of the capitalist axiomatic.

Unlike Savage society, where as we have seen "traits of expression . . . follow a machinic phylum and wed it in a distribution of singularities," the capitalist axiomatic "constitutes a form of expression that subjugates the phylum . . . [which] is no longer anything more than an equalized, homogenized, compared content, while expression becomes a form of . . . appropriation" (1987, 444–45). And where the machinic phylum followed by savage expression is composed of flows of matter and energy on the earth, the equalized, homogenized, compared content subjugated by the capitalist form of expression is composed of flows of matter and energy on the extended multiplicity of the global capitalist market—decoded flows that, when registered as prices on the intensive recording surface of the market, get axiomatized for the appropriation of surplus value to pay the infinite debt. A postcapitalist axiomatic would constitute a very different form of expression for the content of the worldwide market: one that would (1) eliminate what I have here called the slope of the market by canceling the infinite debt and replacing central banking with institutions such as credit unions and community banks where debts are mobile, transient and horizontal; and (2) replace wage slavery and the private appropriation of surplus with self-valorizing forms of work and collective appropriation—thereby freeing the production and consumption taking place on the underside of the market surface from any standardization operating in the service of private surplus accumulation and from the obligation to continually grow to pay back the infinite debt on the top side. So, among the most important results of eliminating the slope of the capitalist market would be reducing the pressure for continual economic growth that is so catastrophic for the environment. In addition, without the pressure of differential accumulation to pay the infinite debt, money in a postcapitalist axiomatic would serve as an instrument of exchange rather than a means of extracting surplus value—and as an instrument of exchange, money would foster decoding and thereby promote the world-historical development of freedom from repressive codes and overcodes that Deleuze and Guattari in *Anti-Oedipus* referred to as schizophrenia. *A Thousand Plateaus* recast schizophrenia in terms of (among other things) nondenumerable sets and minor politics, both of which are by-products of the axiom-based extended multiplicity of the world market, with its expanded divisions of labor and leisure and enhanced capacities for creation and enjoyment. Only a postcapitalist axiomatic would promote the positive tendencies of the world market while eliminating the perversion of market dynamics by capital. This, I would suggest, is why Deleuze and Guattari insist (1994, 106) that "the market is the only thing that is universal in capitalism" and why, I would add, it is so important to distinguish the capitalist market from the market itself.

Conclusion

> Part of what going forward means to me is telling some really terrible stories about what's going on in the world.
>
> —Anna Tsing, "Conversations on the Plantationocene"

In the chapter of his comparative study of Sade and Masoch titled "Are Sade and Masoch Complementary?," Deleuze recounts a popular joke about "the meeting between a sadist and a masochist; the masochist says: 'Hurt me.' The sadist replies: 'No'" (1971, 40). The point of retelling even as "particularly stupid" (1971, 40) a joke as this, for Deleuze, is to confirm his answer the chapter title's question and the conclusion of the entire study: no, sadism and masochism are not and cannot be complementary. What I have shown here, however, is that there is one context in which Sadism and Masochism are indeed complementary, if only indirectly: that is when they are simultaneously separated from and connected to one another by the capitalist market. In order to produce surplus value, capital Sadistically reduces both human and natural resources to quantifiable factors of production; in order to forestall crises of overproduction/underconsumption and thereby continue to realize and accumulate surplus value, capital turns buyers into Masochistic consumers who fabricate their very sense of self via the goods, services, and lifestyles they are able to purchase and/or induced to imagine purchasing. Without this combination of Sadism and Masochism, capital would be unable to meet its requirement of continued growth ad infinitum.

Schizoanalysis is particularly well suited to address the problem of capital's drive for infinite self-expansion because it is, in a specific sense subsequently developed by Bruno Latour and Jason Moore and others, a "postmodern" approach to the relation between psychodynamics and sociodynamics. Schizoanalysis can be considered postmodern because it understands that psychodynamics and sociodynamics are essentially the same, despite their apparent separation under capitalism, where reproduction has been segregated from production and delegated to the nuclear family: "Molar social production [sociodynamics] and molecular desiring-production [psychodynamics] must be evaluated both from the viewpoint of their identity in nature and from the viewpoint of their difference in regime" (1983, 336).[1] Along similar lines, Latour (1993) shows that, contrary to modernity's pretense of categorically distinguishing Subject from Object, "we have never been modern," while Moore's critique of modernity shows that "capitalism's dynamism owes much to a specific, and absurd, way of dealing with this relation [between Subject and Object, Society and Nature]: by severing it symbolically, and then acting accordingly" (2015, 21). These views echo Deleuze and Guattari's insistence that they "make no distinction between man and nature: the human essence of nature and the natural essence of man become one within nature in the form of production or industry, just as they do within the life of man as a species" (1983, 4; see also 25: "Nature = Industry, Nature = History"); "social production is desiring-production itself *under determinate* [historical] *conditions*" (1983, 343; original emphasis). Deleuze and Guattari's schizoanalysis of capitalist axiomatics, along with the difference I have elaborated between primary (capitalist) and secondary (legal and scientific) axioms, in fact enables us to make finer distinctions than Moore's blanket critique of modernity allows and to more precisely identify the source of the problem. For there is nothing intrinsically wrong, I would suggest, with equality before the law when it operates as an axiomatic system nor with applying the axioms of basic science to a range of different technologies—both of which can be considered key features, or at least key prospects, of modernity. It is rather the growth imperative entailed by specifically capitalist axioms that produces what he calls "today's biocidal wreckage" (2015, 21).

But Moore's point is well taken. Our civilization—what Deleuze and Guattari in *Anti-Oedipus* (1983, chapter 3) refer to not as capitalist society but as "civilized" society (referring, no doubt, to Freud's view of civilization and its discontents)—whether its emergence is dated to ancient Greece, as Horkheimer and Adorno do; to modernity, as Latour and Moore do; or to whenever the "anthropocene" is thought to begin—this civilization based on infinite growth is rapidly approaching its end. We know this, yet we don't have the institutions to replace it with a new one: we are still awaiting a new axiomatic to replace the capitalist one—another reason Deleuze and

Guattari can be considered postmodern since they insist that schizoanalysis has no blueprint for postcapitalist society or even a political program to offer (1983, 380).[2] What they do offer is a critical understanding of how capitalism operates as an axiomatic system, and, as I have added, how capital perverts the psychodynamics and sociodynamics of markets that might otherwise become free markets.

There is, finally, a third sense in which Deleuze and Guattari's philosophy can be considered postmodern, which is no doubt the most important. Schizoanalysis categorically assigns priority to desire over interests: "Unconscious libidinal investment is what causes us to look for our interest in one place rather than another, to fix our aims on a given path, convinced that this is where our chances lie—since love drives us on" (1983, 345). The project of modernity centrally involved subordinating desire—considered irrational—to rational interests, and (in Weber's terms) replacing traditional and charismatic social authority with rational, legal authority. Modernity's failure to do so is perhaps nowhere more dramatically evident than in the election of Donald Trump to the presidency of the United States in 2016. Increasingly widespread precarity engineered by neoliberal capitalism made white supremacists (reacting against civil rights and diversity policies) and Christian supremacists (reacting against reproductive rights and growing secularism) resonate with what I have called "populist supremacism" to produce a cult of personality focused on a borderline-narcissist leader promising (like the defeated German and Confederate officers of the nineteenth and twentieth centuries before him) to reverse their defeats—in his case to restore America to its former glory and disaffected Americans to their rightful social station and position of power over people of color, immigrants, atheists, and women.[3]

At the time of this writing, it is not clear whether or not the "modernist parenthesis" (Latour 2013, 10) has indeed closed—whether or not, that is to say, the rational, legal social authority of the Justice Department will prevail over the charismatic social authority of Trump. His reelection in 2024 would probably confirm that the modernist parenthesis has indeed closed. But it is also conceivable that Trump could be jailed for his crimes and that after taking back the House of Representatives, Democrats could replace neoliberal precarity with a Green New Deal (Klein 2019) based on modern monetary theory (Kelton 2020) and thereby foster polymorphous narcissism rather than borderline supremacism. For even though desire according to schizoanalysis is always primary with respect to interest, which "always comes after" (1983, 346), schizoanalysis also insists that desire is always socially engineered—that social production is nothing other than desiring production under determinate historical conditions. Hence the importance of clearly distinguishing the positive potential of free markets from the actual perversion of markets by capital.

Anthropologists and historians alike have long highlighted critical differences between capitalist markets and noncapitalist markets.[4] Economists often construe the contrast in terms of the difference between "price takers" and "price makers." In truly free "free markets," everyone is a price taker: noone is in a position to set prices unilaterally; it is the market dynamics of supply and demand that set prices. As market competition centralizes capital in fewer and fewer private hands, however, price makers emerge who are able to set prices unilaterally.[5] (Antitrust legislation represents a—mostly failed—attempt to prevent this outcome.) This is particularly true—and particularly detrimental—in the labor market, where unemployment is generally maintained at a level that effectively allows employers to keep the price of labor low enough to ensure profitability. (In the absence of full-employment policy, unions represent a—mostly failed—attempt to prevent this outcome.) Little attention has been paid, however, to the psychodynamics of markets and the dramatic contrast between the psychodynamics of capitalist and noncapitalist markets.

This study builds on previous psychoanalytically informed social psychologies that share the premise that social factors determine individual psychology rather than the other way around—notably the work of Wilhelm Reich and Herbert Marcuse. Yet the work of Norman O. Brown, despite his inveterate psychologism, is also important—for providing an account of "the psychoanalytical meaning of history," by which he means an explanation for the relentless expansion of production and consumption known as "progress." Because caregivers inevitably frustrate the unrealistic expectations of childhood, according to Brown, human beings repress the death instinct and are driven to produce and consume more and more in an unconscious attempt to satisfy rather than relinquish those expectations. What Brown leaves out of his account is the psychoanalytic concept of *Nachträglichkeit*, along with the fact that capital exacerbates whatever degree of dissatisfaction that may or may not exist in childhood by frustrating even the most realistic of expectations in adulthood. For capital represses the death instinct by focusing inexorably on accumulating surplus value at the expense of enjoyment, on stockpiling means (of production) rather than expending and enjoying ends.[6] In this context, Reich's contribution is salutary for he insists that frustrations imposed by the superego only apparently originate in parental authority figures: they actually serve as relays for the boss and the capitalist ruling class as a whole. Yet Reich's explanatory recourse to ruling class oppression doesn't take into account the disavowal of social authority in Masochism, which is key to understanding the extraordinary flexibility of capital and its ability to recuperate political resistance through the identity politics of consumerism. Here, Marcuse's concept of "repressive desublimation" provides a useful description of one aspect of the psychodynamics of Masochist consumerism: the desublimation required for ever-increasing levels of consumption remains repressive because purchasing consumer goods fuels the private appropriation of surplus value and thereby increases the power of capital over markets and society at large.[7]

Lacan's linguistic version of psychoanalysis comes to a similar conclusion, albeit from different premises. For Lacan, it is the loss of the object to the signifier, rather than the process of weaning, that propels the subject into a vain and endless search to reclaim the lost object and establish an identity that feels whole. What Marcuse called "repressive desublimation" appears from this perspective as surplus enjoyment. But here, too, the Freudian concept of *Nachträglichkeit* is crucial: for objects are not really lost to signification; they are actively taken from us by the relations of production of capitalism. So even though the relation to objects may well be attenuated by meaning, whatever loss that entails is exacerbated *nachträglich* by the theft of what Marxists call our "objective being" and by the corollary obligation to buy back from capital the products of our labor—at a price that is always just out of reach: a trauma that gets renewed and intensified by each and every one of the myriad advertisements we are subjected to on a daily—or hourly—basis. But the Lacanian superego imperative to "Enjoy!" turns out to be only half the picture: in order to enjoy yourself more (as a consumer), you have to deny yourself more (as a producer)—which only aggravates the splitting of the subject of language and can lead to borderline conditions and even schizophrenia.

Meanwhile, Marcuse's earlier concepts (1955, especially chapter 10)—positive narcissism, polymorphous perversity, and nonrepressive sublimation—retain much of their critical, utopian force. Yet where Marcuse attributes the prospects for noninstrumental relations with the environment and greater variety in socially acceptable modes of instinctual gratification to the "conquest of scarcity," it is important to recognize with Deleuze and Guattari the extent to which these and other positive prospects are in fact facilitated by the development of the world market—once freed from its subsumption by capital. This understanding of what makes a "free market" free is the obverse of what free-market ideologues mean by the term: it means freedom from the power of capital, not freedom from regulation by the state. Indeed, the notion that markets could function without state intervention is a either a smokescreen or a delusion: markets always have been and always will be constituted and regulated by sets of rules, both legal and customary (Finn 2006; Graeber 2011; Pistor 2019). Moreover, far from being free from state regulation, capitalist markets are in fact and always have been structured by the state to systemically favor capital over other social interests (Pistor 2019). So the real question is whether markets will be structured to incentivize antisocial and antienvironmental behavior, as they are under capitalism, or to foster greater equality, social cooperation, and environmental protection.[8] So it is not only under capitalism that the struggle around axioms is important: a postcapitalist axiomatic will also entail establishing and continually revising through jurisprudence what I have called "secondary" or state axioms to ensure that primary axioms of the market operate sustainably in the service of the common good.[9]

Eliminating the power of capital over markets is important because when social relations are based primarily on market exchange (that is to say, on axiomatics), decoding frees experience from preestablished, socially imposed meanings and rules—from the constraints of what Marcuse (1969) called "administered society" and Foucault (1979) called "normalization."[10] Basing social relations on market exchange can also undermine social authority, favoring ego-ideal emulation over superego punishment. Of course, emulation in itself is no panacea: bad role models can be emulated instead of good ones, just as superego prohibitions can themselves be good or bad. But emulation is the more promising form of socialization, inasmuch as it is based on shared positive ideals rather than imposed negative proscriptions. Finally, the development of the world market accelerates the divisions of labor and leisure, vastly increasing the variety of modes of coping and gratification and thereby providing a vehicle for the acceptance and social integration of greater degrees of neurodiversity and what Marcuse and Brown called polymorphous perversity. Market exchange enhances diversity and freedom by turning us away (*per-vertere*) from preestablished modes of coping and gratification to share and experiment with new and different modes in production and consumption alike. That is why rescuing the (immanent) multiplicity of the world market from its (quasitranscendent) capture by capital is so important, and why, I would suggest, Deleuze and Guattari insist that the market is the only thing that is universal in capitalism.[11]

But this kind of market-based perversity must be distinguished from the perversions induced through markets by capital, which are the focus of this book. Given the primacy of finance capital over productive capital, capitalist markets are oriented primarily to the repayment of debt—a debt that is infinite inasmuch as capital accumulation is endless, in both senses of the term. Capital thereby transforms the temporary turning away from immediate gratification for the sake of enhanced and diversified modes of ulterior gratification that inheres in markets into a permanent turning away that subordinates gratification by prioritizing the endless production and private accumulation of surplus value over the collective production and enjoyment of wealth. One result of this perversion of perversity is that the capitalist economy must perpetually grow—a requirement that we now know, but must explicitly acknowledge, is leading to the end of civilization as we know it.[12] Another result is the imposition of a binary, vertical power hierarchy on the horizontal network of multiple differential relations comprising the world market itself. Yet another result of subordinating gratification to accumulation is the aggravation of separation anxiety through generalized precarity, which intensifies the repetition compulsion to the point that it subsumes the pleasure principle.[13] Limiting gratification prevents people from developing new modes of coping, locking them into preestablished modes; where the perversity of the market multiplies and diversifies modes of coping and gratification, capitalist perversion produces fixations, with repetition determining what is found to be pleasurable, rather than pleasure determining what may be repeated. Through its perversion of perversity and the imposition of austerity, capital introduces two layers of perversion into the psychodynamics of the market: Sadism and Masochism. Formally, sadism is pleasure in torture endlessly repeated, while masochism is pleasure by torture repeatedly deferred. And it is not just their psychodynamic form but also the content of the classic perversions that offer critical diagnoses of the problems in production and consumption specific to the capitalist market.

Incarnated in material as well as discursive practices, Sadism reduces everything qualitative to quantified factors of production. The mathematized epistemologies initiated by Galileo, Descartes, and Locke enable the translation of artisanal know-how (*savoir-faire*) into abstract knowledge (*connaissance*), which then gets reintroduced as technology into the production process to make it more efficient, subordinating labor to management in the process. Labor power itself becomes an abstract commodity, with wages paid according to the amount of time worked rather than the amount or quality of the goods actually produced. The combination of technological enhancement, time-based wage labor, and improved mathematical notation culminates in the sacrifice of substantive wealth and its enjoyment to abstract value and its endless accumulation, just as the secondary characters in Sadean discourse are sacrificed to the endlessly repeated pleasures of the primary characters. By making the production and accumulation of surplus value its primary aim, capital shifts focus away from ends to means—to producing ever more means of production as capital rather than enhancing consumption. And as even privatized consumption itself becomes a factor of production of surplus value, consumers seek to compensate for being treated as factors of production via Masochistic consumerism: "Living well," so the saying goes, "is the best revenge." As the second layer of perversion, Masochism reacts to the Sadism of capitalist production relations by disavowing social authority and fabricating an idealized identity based on consumerism—initially located in the private domestic sphere as diagnosed in Masochean discourse and then becoming more widespread as the domestic sphere gets absorbed by predatory marketing in a mass-mediated, administered society. By contracting to suffer domination willingly in private rather than confront it in public, the Masochist ends up getting the goods, so to speak. But even this apparent, and in any case temporary, success via consumerism turns against them by contributing directly to the realization and accumulation of surplus value and thereby increasing the power of capital over production and consumption alike. Capitalism is, moreover, Masochistic in its very temporality: overproducing means (of production) requires and results in indefinite deferral of enjoying ends.[14]

As the growth imperative imposed on markets by capital drives production and consumption farther and farther apart and multiplies modes of coping and gratification, borderline conditions eclipse the perversions of Sadism and Masochism as the predominant form of market psychodynamics, with mixed results. Instead of locking people into fixed modes of gratification, market-induced separation anxiety (precarity) now compels them to continually reinvent, diversify, and enjoy themselves—as private consumers.[15] Alongside the positive potential for neurodiversity and polymorphous narcissism mentioned above, there are two, more problematic responses to the late-capitalist market: secondary narcissism and supremacism. Most cultural critics and historians have focused on narcissism and on the ways it undermines social bonds and pits isolated individuals against one another and society at large. But the psychodynamics of borderline supremacism are if anything even more troubling, combining remnants of Masochism in its absolute submission to a chosen authority with remnants of Sadism in its punitive relation to vulnerable others. Those whom capitalist austerity threatens to deprive of their once-established identities—their lifestyles, income-streams, and positions in society—are inclined by the slope of the market to identify with a revered authority figure and become increasingly anxious to punish those perceived as gaining what they feel they themselves have lost or are at risk of losing.[16]

Capitalist austerity has in the past come in waves or cycles; indeed, Keynesian economic policy was expressly designed to mitigate "cyclical downturns" in the economy through government deficit spending and may have helped forestall the spread of populist and other supremacisms in the midtwentieth century. What is certain is that postwar prosperity ("les trente glorieuses") spawned a whole set of important social justice movements, including the civil rights, women's rights, environmental, and peace movements. Neoliberalism, however—aimed precisely against Keynesianism and government spending on social programs—threatens to make austerity permanent and has already contributed to making what I have called "populist supremacism" more virulent and widespread throughout the world. Although capital cannot be considered the cause of problems such as racism, homophobia, ethnocentrism, nativism, and misogyny, capitalist austerity does serve as a key enabling condition and provides a resonance chamber for these other forms of supremacism, and their mutually reinforcing psychodynamics make them all the more toxic.[17] There are of course many ways of addressing social problems such as racism, homophobia, and misogyny, but given how pervasive capitalism is, freeing markets from capital's perversion of perversity must be counted among them and may be among the most important.

The problem of which capital *can* be considered the principal cause, however, is the environmental crisis, including mass extinctions, habitat destruction, ocean acidification, widespread pollution, and most dramatically, global warming. When investment capital captures and dominates markets, more value must be produced than was originally loaned so as to pay back the loan with interest: endless accumulation to repay the infinite debt. In order to continually produce more value, capital Sadistically treats all planetary resources—both natural and human—as mere factors of production: Mother Earth gets repeatedly raped for natural resources, and human beings get stripped of their natural sociality and reduced to their individual labor power and purchasing power. But capital's Sadistic fixation on the production of surplus value results in chronic crises of overproduction, to which privatized Masochistic consumerism responds by compensating for capital's theft of purchasing power with the fabrication of imaginary consumer identities spiked with seething resentment. Surplus repression for the sake of ever-increasing production conjoins on the capitalist market with surplus enjoyment for the sake of ever-increasing consumption, fueling a megamachine devoted to endless accumulation. It has been said that imagining the end of life on earth is easier than imagining the end of capitalism. But we don't have to imagine the end of life: we are seeing it daily as species after species goes extinct, and we can easily see that it's getting worse. Imagining the end of capitalism may require, as Mike Davis (2018, 320) has argued, "a return to explicitly utopian thinking," but such thinking, he continues, must include "a new willingness to advocate the Necessary rather than the merely Practical"—or the purely Ideal. Ending capitalism may seem utopian, but it has become absolutely Necessary—not just for the betterment of the human condition, but for very survival of life as we know it on this planet.

Notes

Part One Introduction

1. In using the psychoanalytic concept of *Nachträglichkeit* to assert the priority of the afterward over the initial, of social over purely psychic determinations, I am translating into a more familiar idiom what Deleuze and Guattari in *Anti-Oedipus* critique under the rubric of the "fifth paralogism of psychoanalysis: the afterward" (1983, 126–30; Holland 1999, 55–57). From the critique of this paralogism, they conclude that "psychic repression is a means in the service of social repression" (1983, 119). In *A Thousand Plateaus*, Deleuze and Guttari complain that "the human sciences, with their materialist, evolutionary, and even dialectical schemas, lag behind the richness and complexity of causal relations in physics [and] biology," and go on to praise physics and biology for "present[ing] us with reverse causalities that are without finality but testify nonetheless to an action of the future on the present, or of the present on the past, for example, the convergent wave and the anticipated potential, which imply an inversion of time" (1987, 431): I take *Nachträglichkeit* to be a kind of reverse causality. Freud discusses the concept as early as his "Project for a Scientific Psychology" (1953, vol. 1), and returns for a more in-depth discussion in "Remembering, Repeating, and Working-Through" (1953, vol. 12).

2. As Deleuze (1971, 37) says of Sade's and Masoch's use of sexualization and exaggeration, "eroticism is able to act as a mirror to the world by reflecting its excesses, drawing out its violence and even confering a 'spiritual' quality on these phenomena."

3. I am not claiming that this is "the meaning" of Sade's or Masoch's texts, although there is ample evidence to support this kind of claim (Casilli 1996). Instead, I am following Deleuze's kind of reading strategy, according to which "a text is merely a small cog in an extratextual practice. It is not a question of commentating [*sic*] on the text. . . . [I]t is a question of seeing what *use* it has in the extra-textual practice that prolongs the text" (Deleuze 1997, xvi; original emphasis). The apparent opposition between these two kinds of reading is dispelled if we agree with Wittgenstein (1953, §§ 139, 197) that "meaning is use."

4. Masochism has proven much harder than sadism to square with Freud's pleasure principle, but see Glick and Meyers (1988), Baumeister (1989), Hanly (1995), and Noyes (1997).

5. The contrast between Sade's and Masoch's literary works in what follows is based on Gilles Deleuze's comparative study (Deleuze 1971), whose polemical aim is to show, contra the sexological and psychoanalytic reductions, that sadism and masochism are incompatible and not simple inversions of one another. In emphasizing the form of these literary works, I agree with Anna Kornbluh that "there are heartier things to be affirmed about literature than the affects it arouses in individuals. Literary form is more social than that" (Kornbluh 2017, 398); I am not concerned with finding a utopian element in these literary works, however, as Kornbluh generally recommends.

6. Regarding the historical contexts of these literary works, Deleuze only briefly hints at political events rather than economic developments: "As against [Sade's] ironic conception of the institution based on the rejection of law and contract, and in the context of the Revolution of 1789, we have to consider the humorous contribution of Masoch and his conception of the relationship between the contract and the law, in the context of the 1848 Revolution" (1971, 78–79; see also 37–38).

7. Contrasting the original literary discourses of sadism and masochism distances this project from various attempts in psychoanalysis to define perversion in terms of desire's vicissitudes (Freud) or structure (Lacan), most of which fall prey to the "reversibility" thesis according to which sadism and masochism are simply inversions of one another—as when James Penney, following Lacan, says of perversion that its "structure effectively allows the subject to cause his own enjoyment in the Other, and thereby to function at the same time, however vicariously, as both sadist and masochist" (Penney 2006, 19; see also Lacan 1989). The only time Sadism and Masochism can function together, I will show, is when their otherwise incompatible dynamics are conjoined by the intermediation of the market.

8. See Marx and Engels (1975, vol. 35, chapters 27 and 28).

Chapter One

1. First article of the second part of the *Smalcald Articles* (Luther 2017).

2. This is not to say that sodomy itself cannot be pleasurable, but only that it is represented in Sadean discourse as a sterile means of inflicting pain and/or humiliation.

3. Sade's *Juliette* (1797) is generally taken to be a response to Rousseau's *Julie, ou la nouvelle Héloïse* (1761).

4. Kant says:

In the immeasurableness of nature and the incompetence of our faculty for adopting a standard proportionate to the aesthetic estimation of the magnitude of its realm, we found our own limitation. But with this we also found in our rational faculty another non-sensuous standard, one which has that infinity itself under it as a unit, and in comparison with which everything in nature is small, and so found in our minds a pre-eminence over nature even in it immeasurability. Now in just the same way the irresistibility of the might of nature forces upon us the recognition of our physical helplessness as beings of nature, but at the same time reveals a faculty of estimating ourselves as independent of nature, and discovers a pre-eminence above nature. (2007, § 28)

5. Bacon, *Valerius Terminus: of the Interpretation of Nature*, cited in Horkheimer and Adorno (1972, 5).

6. It had been identified as such as early as Cicero. In 1767, the French journalist Simon Linguet published an influential description of wage slavery:

The slave was precious to his master because of the money he had cost him . . . They were worth at least as much as they could be sold for in the market . . . It is the impossibility of living by any other means that compels our farm labourers to till the soil whose fruits they will not eat and our masons to construct buildings in which they will not live . . . It is want that compels them to go down on their knees to the rich man in order to get from him permission to enrich him . . . [W]hat effective gain [has] the suppression of slavery brought [him?] He is free, you say. Ah! That is his misfortune. . . . These men . . . [have] the most terrible, the most imperious of masters, that is, need. . . . They must therefore find someone to hire them, or die of hunger. Is that to be free?" (cited in Marx and Engels 1969, 440)

7. Until 1972, state banks had indirect recourse to precious metal in the sense that they were supposed to have a gold or silver reserve to back up the paper money they issued. Even that convenient fiction was dispensed with when Nixon took the US dollar off the gold standard altogether; other state banks quickly followed suit. See Di Muzio and Robbins (2016).

8. While Roman numerals were used for notation, the abacus was used for calculation; as a physical counting system, it suffered the same material limitations as iconic marks, however, compared to the notation systems that replaced it.

9. Raising a number to the power of two or three (squaring or cubing) was known to the ancient Greeks; Nicole Oresme (1323–82), Nicolas Chuquet (1445–88), and Michael Stifel (1487–1567) are usually credited with expanding

exponentiation indefinitely beyond the second and third powers; by Decartes's time, the use of superscript to designate exponentiation was widely known.

10. Naomi Klein summarizes:

> Alongside the theories that rationalized treating humans as raw capitalist assets to exhaust and abuse without limit were theories that justified treating the natural world (forests, rivers, land and water animals) in precisely the same way. Millennia of accumulated human wisdom about how to safeguard and regenerate everything from forests to fish runs were swept away in favor of a new idea that there was no limit to humanity's ability to control the natural world, nor to how much wealth could be extracted from it without fear of consequence. (2019, 30)

11. M-C-M' becomes more important than C-M-C' in the customary shorthand for investments and commercial transactions, respectively, where M stands for money, C and C' stand for different commodities (sold and purchased respectively), and M' for an increased amount of money.

12. Cited in Perelman (2013), who actually refers to Volcker's policy as "sadomonetarism." About "those who praise Volcker [and] like to say he 'broke the back' of inflation," Tim Barker suggests that "Reagan's economic adviser Michael Mussa was nearer the truth when he said that 'to establish its credibility, the Federal Reserve had to demonstrate its willingness to spill blood, lots of blood, other people's blood'" (2019).

13. Cited in Oppel (2004).

14. In his critique of specifically capitalist markets, Raj Patel puts the point this way:

> This is not to say that the people who work in these [corporations] are vicious or cruel or callous. I recently debated Unilever's director of sustainable agriculture, Jan Kees Vis, by all accounts a decent, committed, thoughtful and caring man, trying to do right by the planet. He oversees many initiatives that benefit both the planet and his company—saving water, using less fossil fuel and so on. But as he admitted, the minute that he adopts a policy that benefits the environment but harms the company is the minute he will lose his job. (2010, 43)

It is capitalist market forces, in other words, that compel otherwise "decent" people to be Sadistic.

15. Elucidating the real conditions enabling the emergence of a phenomenon such as capitalism (or any phenomenon) is the hallmark of Deleuze's "transcendental empiricism," his critical transformation of Kant's transcendental idealism; see Bryant (2008).

16. Mapping the totality of social conditions, according to Weber, would involve showing

> the significance of ascetic rationalism, which has only been touched in the foregoing sketch, for the content of practical social ethics, thus for the types of organization and the functions of social groups from the conventicle to the State. Then its relations to humanistic rationalism, its ideals of life and cultural influence; further to the development of philosophical and scientific empiricism, to technical development and to spiritual ideals would have to be analysed. Then its historical development from the medieval beginnings of worldly asceticism to its dissolution in pure utilitarianism would have to traced out through all the areas of ascetic religion. Only then could the quantitative cultural significance of ascetic Protestantism in its relation to other plastic elements of culture be estimated. (Weber 1958, 182–83)

17. According to Weber:

> In fact, the summum bonum of this [the Protestant] ethic, the earning of more and more money, combined with the strict avoidance of all spontaneous enjoyment of life, is above all completely devoid of any eudaemonistic, not to say hedonistic, admixture. It is thought of so purely as an end in itself, that from the point of view of the happiness of, or utility to, the single individual, it appears entirely transcendental and absolutely irrational. Man is dominated by the making of money, by acquisition as the ultimate purpose of his life. Economic acquisition is no longer subordinated to man as the means for the satisfaction of his material needs. This reversal of what we should call the natural relationship, so irrational from a naive point of view, is evidently as definitely a leading principle of capitalism as it is foreign to all peoples not under capitalistic influence. (1958, 53)

18. The dangers of neoliberalism are made abundantly clear in Wendy Brown's *Undoing the Demos* (2015), where she adroitly combines insights from both Foucault and Marx.

19. "Victorious capitalism, since it rests on mechanical foundations, needs [the support of Protestant asceticism] no longer" (Weber 1958, 181–82).

20. In this respect, modern state citizenship can also be considered masochistic, reinforcing the Masochism of contemporary capitalist consumerism; on the double-edged sword of rights claims, see Wendy Brown (1995).

21. See Barbara Mennel (2001), who suggests that undue emphasis on the psychology of masochism in Masoch's domestic novels has obscured the importance

of his extensive output of historical novels. The focus here on the diagnostic thrust of his domestic fiction is not meant to imply that it is necessarily also true of the historical novels, although they do share many main themes (the centrality of strong women, the dynamics of trust and betrayal, and others). Masochism in the modern European novel is widely recognized; see inter alia Massé (1992), Stewart-Steinberg (1998), Noble (2000), Kucich (2007), and Jarvis (2016).

22. The quotation continues: "In our work we may be superior to them. . . . But vis-à-vis a woman we love, believe me, all this morbid ambition is forgotten. There we become soft and simple and turn into children who love to be spoilt and put our heads in your lap while you tell us beautiful dreams" (Andreas-Salomé 1990, 75).

23. By contrast, serfs owed fealty, along with a variable proportion of their product, to their feudal lords, but they retained sovereignty over their work. Some post-Lacanians have also noted the capitalist privatization of subjectivity: "The increasing privatization that has occurred after capitalism's emergence is a direct product of the logic of capitalism. The more subjects become subjects of capitalism, the more they turn away from public space and seek refuge in their private worlds" (McGowan 2016, 51).

24. Of course, one can also consume in order to signal belonging to a group, which is just a different way of using consumption to establish identity.

25. "Suspense" is widely recognized to be central to the Victorian novel because of its relation to the peculiar temporal structure of capitalism: products' economic value is produced in production, but only realized when they are bought back from the capitalist, while their psychological value may be variably realized when they are imagined, purchased, and/or consumed (Karatani 2003). Critics vary as to whether Victorian novels merely reflect, promote, or actively critique this temporal structure. See Lynch (1998), Levine (2003), Lesjak (2006), Poovey (2008), Kornbluh (2014), and Thorsteinsson (2016).

26. As Deleuze says, "Masoch is the writer who makes suspense, in its pure and almost unbearable state, the motivating force of the novel" (1997, 54).

27. In addition to Deleuze's study of Masoch (1971), see Theodor Reik (1941), upon whom Deleuze draws.

28. It could be argued that labor contracts aren't really entered into willingly; that having no other means of life in fact forces workers to accept the conditions of wage labor out of necessity, whatever the mitigating effects of labor contracts on those conditions might be. And that is simply true. But the rhetoric, the legal status, and the common understanding of the labor contract nonetheless presume the free will of both parties, notwithstanding the obfuscation regarding the role of necessity, and it is the labor contract so understood that becomes the object of Masochean parody.

29. On the two circuits of money, see Deleuze and Guattari (1983, 228–30) and Suzanne de Brunhoff (1971).

30. The cataclysmic conclusion of the Masochean narrative does not figure in Deleuze's analysis of the Masochean scenario (1971), but it is crucial in disclosing the instability of Masochism and its tendency to precipitate borderline conditions.

Chapter Two

1. See Jacoby (1983). The Lacanian idiom for such psychic fragmentation is "le corps morcelé"; see the "Mirror Stage" essay in Lacan (2006, 75–81).

2. Kiarina Kordela argues that contemporary "informatized" capitalism exploits leisure at least as much as labor: "Today's informatized capitalism obtains unforeseen dimensions of economic exploitation, as well as of conformism, because it is the first era that has succeeded in maximizing its affective exploitation due to the colonization of the means of subsistence (including leisure) by the means of production (information). Put simply, maximum economico-affective exploitation succeeds because we play with the same materials during our so-called leisure time that we use during our so-called work time" (2023, 52).

3. Deleuze suggests that advanced forms of "control" capitalism target these partial sevles or "dividuals" rather than whole individuals (1992, 180–82).

4. See Buchen (2009). Recent research (Luck 2019; Hahn 2022) suggests that recognition failure alternates with hyperfocus in some schizophrenics.

5. According to Kernberg (1975), not all borderlines are narcissistic, but nearly all narcissists are borderline.

6. Thirty years after its appearance, the antihero of Ellis's novel, far from losing its relevance, has become the hero of an entire internet subculture (Yalcinkaya 2002; Rex 2023).

7. The dynamic of punitive projective identification remains central to recent updates of Adorno and colleagues' analysis, such as that of Robert Altemeyer (1996), who reduces the original nine character traits of the authoritarian personality to three: conventionalism, submissiveness, and aggressiveness.

8. See his "Remarks on *The Authoritarian Personality*" (2016); the remarks were originally meant to conclude the book, but weren't included. The combination of submissiveness and aggressiveness is what allowed Erich Fromm (1976) to call the authoritarian personality "sadomasochistic," in the reductive Freudian sense of the term.

9. "We are convinced that the ultimate source of prejudice has to be sought in social factors which are incomparably stronger than the "psyche" of any one individual involved. . . . Our detailed analysis of subjective patterns does not mean that, in our opinion, prejudice can be explained in such terms. On the contrary, we regard the analysis of objective social forces which engender prejudice as the most pressing issue in contemporary research into anti-minority bias" (Adorno 2016, 2).

10. The intense gratification and even joy of being among other people who are supposed to believe exactly as you do is an often-ignored factor in the appeal of Trumpism, experienced with particular intensity at his rallies and the boat parades held in his honor (French 2023).

11. The fact of rising income and wealth inequality in America is well known; a RAND Corporation study (Price and Edwards 2020) estimates that $50 trillion have been transferred from working- and middle-class Americans to the super rich since the last quarter of the twentieth century.

12. Along with white supremacism and Christian nationalism, populist supremacism was a major factor in Donald Trump ascending to the US presidency in 2017. For confirmation of the pathological narcissism and borderline supremacism of Trump, see Lee (2019).

13. Psychoanalytically informed cultural criticism appeared almost immediately after the first modern clinical definitions of narcissism were formulated by Heinz Kohut (1971) and Otto Kernberg (1975): among the early social commentary articles were Peter Marin's "The New Narcissism" (1975) and Tom Wolfe's "The 'Me' Decade and the Third Great Awakening" (1976); see also Clecak (1983). For a critical review, see Battan, who argues that "while Lasch has tainted [social] changes with images of social chaos and mental disorder—the elimination of the individual's sense of moral responsibility, the mindless pursuit of hedonistic self gratification, and the subsequent decline of the work ethic, the nuclear family and political democracy—others . . . by shifting their interpretive framework, have identified the same phenomena as healthy, adaptive responses to contemporary social and economic changes that will ultimately revitalize American culture" (1983, 209). Among those who analyze cultural narcissism in a positive light from a psychoanalytic perspective, see Malcolm (1971), whose major drawback is to construe positive narcissism as characteristic of entire generation, rather than as one late-capitalist basin of attraction among several.

14. Updating Weber for the twentieth century, Sennett calls narcissism the "protestant ethic of modern times" (1974, 333).

15. In a similar vein, Leo Bersani proposes that narcissism can provide the basis for a relationship to others that is ego-dissolving rather than ego-centric, in what he calls "impersonal narcissism" (Bersani and Phillips 2008, especially chapter 3).

16. It is in this sense that Marcuse (1955) maintains that the relation of primary narcissism to the external world is—at least partially—an erotic one.

17. On Deleuze and Guattari's relations to Klein and Lacan regarding the concept of partial objects, see Beckman (2013, especially chapter 2).

18. Marcuse and Brown drew on Freud's characterization of infant sexuality as "polymorphously perverse" (*Standard Edition*, vol. 7, 191).

19. The distinction between perversity and perversion can be traced to Freud but becomes more explicit in Lacan and post-Lacanians: James Penney, for example,

insists that "a fundamental conceptual distinction must be drawn between desire's essential perversity and perversion as such" (2006, 1).

20. Scholars such as Bataille (1988), Mauss (2002), and Davis (2018) argue in favor of social or public consumption rather than the privatized form, which is a key component of consumer Masochism.

Part Two Introduction

1. On the use Deleuze and Guattari make of concepts from Marx and Nietzsche in their critical transformation of psychoanalysis into schizoanalysis, see Holland (1999, viii, 4–23).

2. For simplicity's sake, I retain the term *schizoanalysis* even while drawing extensively on concepts from *A Thousand Plateaus* (Deleuze and Guttari 1987) and *What Is Philosophy?* (Deleuze and Guattari 1994).

3. "The war machine [as] the invention of the nomad . . . is in its essence the constitutive element of smooth space . . . and the corresponding composition of people: this is its sole and veritable positive object" (Deleuze and Guattari 1987, 417).

4. To be clear, Kornbluh herself is careful not to level this charge against schizoanalysis, but against "neo-Deleuzianisms and neo-Spinozisms such as those of Hardt and Negri" (2019, 19), among others.

5. Kiarina Kordlela (2023), however, draws on Spinoza to argue that Marx's category of labor-power can itself address the intensified rate and expanded range of objects of exploitation in what she calls the "informatized era" of contemporary capitalism.

6. Deleuze and Guattari argue that the "isomorphy" of the "international capitalist axiomatic. . . . tolerates [or] in fact . . . requires a certain peripheral polymorphy" of productive processes (1987, 436). For a demonstration of how widely such "pericapitalist" productive processes can vary, see Tsing (2015).

7. However, in a later work, Deleuze explains the philosophical adaptation of concepts from science this way: "We realize the dangers of citing scientific propositions outside their own sphere. It is the danger of arbitrary metaphor or of forced application. But perhaps these dangers are averted if we restrict ourselves to taking from scientific operators a particular conceptualizable character which itself refers to non-scientific areas, and converges with science without applying it or making it a metaphor" (1989, 129). For a fuller explication of the philosophical concept of axiomatics, based on Deleuze's use of Kant and Bergson, see Somers-Hall (2023).

8. On the the relation between concepts and their components, see Deleuze and Guattari (1994, chapter 1); and Paul Patton (2000, especially 12–18).

9. As Deleuze says with respect to Freudian psychoanaysis, "It is not the complex which provides us with information about Oedipus and Hamlet, but

rather Oedipus and Hamlet who provide us with information about the complex" (1990, 237).

10. See also what Deleuze reiterates in returning to the works of Masoch in *Essays Critical and Clinical*: "More a physician than a patient, the writer makes a diagnosis, but what he diagnoses is the world" (1997, 53).

11. This does not mean that authors' and readers' evaluations must agree—on the contrary.

12. This is one sense in which Deleuze and Guattari argue that "a book exists only through the outside and on the outside. A book itself is a little machine . . . [T]he only question is which other machine the literary machine can be plugged into, must be plugged into in order to work" (1987, 4).

Chapter Three

1. Deleuze and Guattari insist on the "identical nature and differing regimes" of psychodynamics and sociodynamics (of desiring production and social production, in their terms) throughout *Anti-Oedipus* (Deleuze and Guattari 1983, especially 28–29, 31–35, 54, 99, 116, 184, 262, 336–37. See also Holland (1999, 19–23, 56, 92).

2. According to Deleuze and Guattari:

> The Marx-Freud parallelism between the two [money and shit] remains utterly sterile and insignificant as long as it is expressed in terms that make them introjections or projections of each other without ceasing to be utterly alien to each other, as in the famous equation money = shit. The truth of the matter is that social production is purely and simply desiring production itself under determinate conditions. We maintain that the social field is immediately invested by desire, that it is the historically determined product of desire, and that libido has no need of any mediation or sublimation, any psychic operation, any transformation, in order to invade and invest the productive forces and the relations of production. (1983, 28–29)

For another discussion of the relation between projection and introjection, see Adorno (1967–68).

3. For both procedures, see chapter 3 of *Anti-Oedipus* (Deleuze and Guattari 1983).

4. "Obey!" and "Enjoy!" may combine to form the kind of double-bind Gregory Bateson argued is conducive to schizophrenia, which if anything would reinforce the schizophrenia produced by decoding according to Deleuze and Guattari; see his "Toward a Theory of Schizophrenia" and "Doube-Bind" (Bateson 1972, 201–27, 271–78).

5. As Karatani puts it, "capital's movement has to continue *endlessly*. Indeed [it] is *interminable* and *without telos*" (2003, 209; original emphasis).

6. On the induction of guilt by the nuclear family and its Oedipus complex, see Deleuze and Guattari (1983, 50, 12–15.)

7. This treatment is what Deleuze and Guattari in *Anti-Oedipus* refer to as the "fifth paralogism of psychoanalysis: the afterward" (1983, 126–30; Holland 1999, 55–57). This paralogism is a special case of the kind of "transcendental illusion" fostered by Kantian idealism, whereby a result of syntheses of apperception—the sense of being a unified "I" actively "having" those perceptions—is mistaken for a precondition of the syntheses (which are passive). In exactly the same way, according to Deleuze and Guattari, a result of production—accumulated capital—not only appears but actually becomes under capitalism the precondition of further production (1983, 225–28). Capitalism is thus in a sense the realization or incarnation of Kantian idealism. This is one reason Deleuze's post-Kantian critique of representation as transcendental illusion is so fruitful as a basis for his understanding and critique of capitalism. On capitalist axiomatics as transcendental illusion, see Somers-Hall (2023).

8. See Brian Rotman (1993, especially 28–32, 54) for a similar argument: mathematics expels the figure of the subject, and a properly mathematical infinity by implication replaces a subjectively figured one.

9. On capital as a continually self-displacing limit, see Deleuze and Guattari: "[C]apitalism . . . has no exterior limit, but only an interior limit that is capital itself and that it does not encounter, but reproduces by always displacing it" (1983, 230–31).

10. As Deleuze and Guattari explain,

> [The] placing of the family outside the social field is . . . the condition under which the entire social field can be applied to the family. Individual persons are social persons first of all, i.e., functions derived from the abstract quantities; they become concrete in the becoming-related or the axiomatic of these quantities, in their conjunction. . . . They are nothing more nor less than . . . the pure "figures" of capitalism; the capitalist as personified capital—i.e., as a function derived from the flow of capital; and the worker as personified labor capacity—i.e., a function derived from the flow of labor. . . . Private persons are therefore images of the second order, images of images—that is, simulacra that are thus endowed with an aptitude for representing the first-order images of social persons. (1983, 264)

11. Capitalism is also characterized by reterritorialization, particularly in the operations of the quasitranscendent nation-state; hence Deleuze and Guattari's struggle to keep philosophical (or "nomadic") thought free from capture by state-supported

and state-supportive thought in its many forms (including Platonism, Hegelianism, et al.).

12. "Father, mother, and child thus become the simulacrum of the images of capital ('Mister Capital, Madame Earth,' and their child the Worker)," where the parental figures appear to dominate even though it is the child who produces value (1983, 264).

13. To which I would add the capture of attention and engagement as sources of surplus value in newer forms of platform, surveillance, and internet capitalism (Srnicek 2016; Zuboff 2019; Ward 2022).

14. On the silence of the death instinct according to Freud, see *Beyond the Pleasure Principle* (1953, vol. 18, 63), where the term is *unobtrusive* rather than silent; *The Ego and the Id* (1953, vol. 19, 46, 59); and *An Outline of Psychoanalysis* (1953, vol. 23, 150).

15. As Deleuze and Guattari put it, "the fixing of the death instinct in fact deprives sexuality of its generative role on at least one essential point, which is the genesis of anxiety, since this genesis becomes the autonomous cause of sexual repression instead of its result; it follows that sexuality as desire no longer animates a social critique of civilization, but that civilization on the contrary finds itself sanctified as the sole agency capable of opposing the death instinct" (1983, 331–32).

16. Imaginary understanding of the Symbolic order and the role of the phallus within it attributes to it a center endowed with more or less absolute authority, while a properly Symbolic understanding construes the phallus as an operator of substitution and semiotic free play; see Lacan (1977) and Holland (1999, 49–52, 90).

17. On the metonymy of desire, see also Holland (1993, 18–19, 162–64, 265–66).

18. These institutions are the object of Foucault's analysis in *Discipline and Punish* (1979).

19. With the advance of decoding, compliance is increasingly enforced via the market and chronic debt rather than disciplinary institutions alone. Compliance enforced by the market is the subject of Foucault's lectures in the *Birth of Biopolitics* (2004b) and Deleuze's essay "Control Society" (1992); see also Lazzarato (2012, 2015) and Brown (2015).

20. It is essential to recognize this source of Deleuze and Guattari's use of the category of schizophrenia, which is subject to considerable disagreement in psychology and psychiatry.

21. Deleuze learned from Bergson (Deleuze 1988) the importance of distinguishing differences of degree (e.g., the attenuation of object relations) from differences of kind (total loss of the object). In this respect, Lacan remains more faithful to Kant (and his "Ding an sich") than Deleuze, who modifies Kant with the help of Nietzsche, among others.

22. About the relation between schizophrenia and decoding, Deleuze and Guattari (1983, 15) say that "the schizophrenic passes from one code to the other, that he deliberately *scrambles all the codes*, by quickly switching from one

to another." See also Nakajima (2019) for neurological evidence supporting this aspect of schizophrenia.

23. They go on to say that "what is missing is not things a subject feels the lack of somewhere deep down inside himself, but rather the objectivity of man, the objective being of man, for whom to desire is to produce, to produce within the realm of the real. The real is not impossible; on the contrary, within the real everything is possible" (1983, 27). It may be that by "impossible" Lacan really means "does not form a totality" (Tomšič 2012, 133), in which case the distance between him and Deleuze and Guattari narrows considerably. But see the proviso in note 29.

24. On primary repression in relation to the "unary trait" in Lacan, see Lacan (1977) and Fink (1995, especially chapter 6); for Deleuze and Guattari's view of primary repression, related to antiproduction and the body without organs, see Deleuze and Guattari (1983, 8–9, 17, 61, 112, 184) and Holland (1999, especially 30–33). For Lacan, primary repression explains the subject's loss of connection to drives upon entry into signification; for Deleuze and Guattari, primary repression is what enables the inscription of desiring production by social production on the body without organs, maintaining a connection between drives and the Real that is not lost but attenuated by codes and overcodes and—in a very different way—by axioms.

25. Karatani says this about capital accumulation and its impact on consumerism: "Far from being motivated by need or desire, [accumulation] is *rooted in perversion* (the opposite of need or desire); and, in reverse, it is [accumulation] that creates in individuals the more-than-necessary need and multifarious desire. . . . [T]he movement of capital . . . does not have a rational motivation. In Freudian terms it is a sort of "compulsion to repeat [*Wiederholungszwang*]" (2003, 210–11; emphasis added). In contrasting capitalists with misers, Karatani here uses "saving" instead of accumulation.

26. About the addictive response to social-media click bait, Dick and McLaughlan suggest that

> such a repetition establishes a development in desire, where it is no longer the wish to access a picture, an update, a rumor—to access the specific object of desire—but desire itself that is the object. . . . With social networks, the human subject is learning to take pleasure in desire itself: not in desire as a pleasurable by-product towards the object, nor even in the only place where it is conceded to be enjoyed as a primary drive, in lack, therefore as a masochistic pleasure. The pleasure—the pay-off—is the effect of desire; it is a learned pleasure, wherein the subject is educated to desire desire itself. (2020, 83)

As I have shown, to defer obtaining the object of desire in order to revel in the resulting suspense is indeed a Masochistic pleasure—the cornerstone in fact of the imaginative hedonism of Masochism, properly understood.

27. Empowering capital is not the only problem with Masochist consumerism: it's also privatized and identity forming. And except for invidious, keeping-up-with-the-Joneses-style consumption, the fabricated identities remain largely independent of one another, even when they are group identities, which they largely and always partly are. But on the production side, on the job market, those group identities are pitted against one another: austerity creates the appearance of a zero-sum game, making everyone compete for resources—in the form of both salaried jobs and state benefits. This feeds identity politics and especially white supremacism, which is not often enough recognized as the epitome of identity politics because it is the "Major" unmarked term, to which all other identities are (invidiously) compared.

28. "Writing in the legacy of Lacan, Todd McGowan avers that the 'rise of the superego and its demand for enjoyment is correlative to the transformation of a society of prohibition to a society of enjoyment' (McGowan 2004, 30). This developmental shift in the superego correlates to advancements in twentieth-century commodity capitalism, with over-production demanding new consumer markets" (Dick and McLaughlan 2020, 144).

29. Lacan's style of discourse is not conducive to assigning just one meaning to a term such as *jouissance* (fixed meaning being considered a form of neurosis in Lacanian psycholinguistics)—and neither is the style of Deleuze and Guattari. *Jouissance* is treated mostly as loss in Lacan's *Seminar* 17 (2007) and as waste in *Seminar* 20 (1998). See also Fink (1995) on the polysemy of the term in Lacan.

30. "Lack (*manque*) is created, planned, and organized in and through social production. . . . It is never primary; production is never organized on the basis of a pre-existing need or lack (*manque*). It is lack that infiltrates itself, creates empty spaces or vacuoles, and propagates itself in accordance with the organization of an already existing organization of production" (Deleuze and Guattari 1983, 28); see also Bataille (1988) and Holland (1999, 31–34, 60–65). As for Bataille, recognition of the primacy of antiproduction over production highlights the importance of making antiproduction enjoyable and collective rather than destructive (militarism) and privatized (consumerism).

Chapter Four

1. Thorstein Veblen is the best-known theorist of the dynamics of conspicuous and invidious consumption (1899), and his critique of the predominance of "business" over "industry" (1904) corresponds to what I here refer to as the precedence of the accumulation of surplus over the production and enjoyment of wealth.

2. The important exception being the axiomatic structuralism of Albert Lautman (1938), on whom Deleuze drew, particularly in chapter 4 of *Difference and Repetition* (1994).

3. This relative consistency is what Althusser (2006) would come to call the perpetual "becoming-necessary" of the capitalist system. Relative consistency in mathematics is different: there it means relative to other axiomatic systems.

4. Here and throughout, I use the terms *intensive* and *extended* (rather than *intensive* and *extensive*) intentionally, in order to analyze the world market both as an extended multiplicity—consisting of actual factories, workers, stores, consumers, and so on arrayed all over the world—and as an intensive multiplicity: a virtual recording surface registering commercial transactions and the investment decisions responsible for the extended market.

5. Russell first treats the measurement of distance in chapter 21, before returning to the topic in chapter 31 (which is the chapter cited by Deleuze and Guattari). In the footnote reference to Russell (1987, 553, n. 15), they warn: "The following discussion does not conform to Russell's theory," but this I would argue is because their notion of "intensive" is derived from Bergson as much as or more than from Russell, and therefore differs significantly from Russell's. For an analysis of Deleuze's terminology in relation to both Russell and Bergson, see Mary Beth Mader (2017, especially 263–68). For an historical account of the rise of measurement accompanying modernity, see Crosby (1997).

6. Russell addresses what I am here calling the "conversion" of nonmetric to metric quantities in these terms: "In order to show that all the distances of our kind . . . can have numbers assigned to them, we require two further axioms, the axiom of Archimedes, and what may be called the axiom of linearity" (1938, 260–61).

7. It might seem that endowing investment capital with a perspective is a form of anthropomorphism, but in Deleuze and Guattari's view, it is capitalist investors who are the personification of investment capital: capitalism is a machine—what Lewis Mumford would call a megamachine—and human beings merely make up some of its working parts; see Deleuze and Guattari (1983, 141) and Mumford (1967).

8. On the asymmetry of the capitalist market, see Kojin Karatani, who explains:

> Those who are in money form (the buyer) and those who are in commodity fonn (the seller) are not symmetric. Those who have money can buy things anytime they want, while those who have commodities have to sell them as soon as possible before they depreciate. Having money is far more advantageous. This becomes conspicuous especially in the relationship between those who have only labor-power commodity and those who buy it with money. This is a free relationship based upon lawful contract, unlike feudal domination and subordination. Yet it is also a hierarchical relationship par excellence, based as it is upon the asymmetric relationship (form) between commodity and money (capital). (2003, 201)

9. This asymmetry between consumers and investors in customarily summarized in two formulae: C-M-C' vs. M-C-M'—presupposing that those I am here calling consumers start with only their labor power, which they sell as a commodity C' in order to obtain money (M) with which to purchase consumer commodities (C'), whereas investors start with money (M) and invest in either goods (mercantile capitalism) or means of production (capitalism proper) in order to accumulate more money (M'). As Karatani puts it, "C'-'-C' and M-'-M' seem like the front and back of the same cycle, but are completely different because the initiative of the circulation is seized and controlled by the possessor of money" (2003, 208).

10. See Deleuze and Guattari (1983, chapter 3) and Holland (1999, 64–68). The difference between surplus value of code and surplus value of flow corresponds to the difference between societies that are organized by coding and overcoding and capitalist society, which is organized by axioms.

11. "'Capital' is not simply another name for means of production; it is means of production reduced to a qualitatively homogeneous and quantitatively measurable fund of value" (Sweezy 1942, 338; cited in Deleuze and Guattari 1987, 569, n. 49).

12. What is required for the world market to function, in other words, is the punctual appearance of homogeneity on the recording surface so that at the time of an investment decision 1 dollar equals precisely 1 dollar or (on July 6, 2022, at 4:38 p.m.) 79 Indian Rupees or 6.70 Chinese Yuan Renminbi.

13. There are serious doubts as to the extent to which so-called reserve ratios really serve as effective limits on the creation of credit money since private banks tend to turn to the central bank to fund their reserves only after loans have already been made. See Di Muzio and Robbins (2016) and Kelton (2020).

14. Nor can money be so plentiful as to raise inflation to the point at which it would effectively cancel out the value of the interest charged.

15. Axioms, Deleuze and Guattari say, are rules that deal "directly with purely functional elements and relations whose nature is not specified, and which are immediately realized in highly varied domains simultaneously" (1987, 454).

16. See Nitzan and Bichler (2009) whose perspective makes it clear that capitalism enslaves two populations rather than one (although as far as I know they themselves do not put it quite this way): not just wage slaves, but also return-on-investment slaves. As Deleuze and Guattari put it, "There are no longer even any masters, but only slaves commanding other slaves" (1983, 254).

17. As Karatani puts it, "The economic phenomenon that appears as the production and consumption of goods contains a veiled, *perverted* drive which is totally different from the ostensible activity. This is the will to M' (M + ΔM)" (2003, 208; emphasis added).

18. See Deleuze and Guattari (1987) plateau 1: "Introduction: Rhizome" and note 4.

19. See Deleuze and Guattari (1987) especially plateau 3: "The Geology of Morals."

20. "In effect, capital acts as the point of subjectification that constitutes all human beings as subjects; but some, the 'capitalists,' are subjects of enunciation that form the private subjectivity of capital, while the others, the 'proletarians,' are subjects of the statement, subjected to the technical machines in which constant capital is effectuated" (Deleuze and Guattari 1987, 457).

21. See Deleuze and Guattari (1983, 237–39) and chapter 1, note 25. Deleuze and Guattari's characterization of capitalist culture as a mix of cynicism and piety corresponds roughly to these two circuits of money and to the two sides of an asymmetrical market surface of which the top, investment side is cynical and Sadistic and the bottom, commercial side is pious and Masochistic (1983, 225).

22. Deleuze and Guattari explain further that

> the *immanent axiomatic* finds in the domains it moves through so many models, termed *models of realization*. It could similarly be said that capital as right, as a "qualitatively homogeneous and quantitatively commensurable element," is realized in sectors and means of production [or that "unified capital" is realized in "differentiated capital"]. However, the different sectors are not alone in serving as models of realization— the States do too. Each of them groups together and combines several sectors, according to its resources, population, wealth, industrial capacity, etc." (1987, 454; emphasis in original)

23. According to Deleuze and Guattari, "What is proper to royal science, to its theorematic or axiomatic power, is to isolate all operations from the conditions of intuition, making them true intrinsic concepts, or 'categories' "(1987, 373).

24. Lacan discusses a similar operation, albeit in Hegelian rather than historical terms, whereby the "slave's" know-how (*savoir-faire*) is translated into the "master's" knowledge (*connaissance*) in *Seminar* 17 (2007, especially 21–22).

25. Drawing on Sohn-Rethel's (1978) conceptualization of "real abstraction" promulgated by market exchange and the political division between intellectual and manual labor, Moore (2015) refers to the world-historical result of this translation as "abstract social nature"—a "systemic family of processes aimed on simplifying, standardizing, and otherwise mapping the world (as external object) in service to the quantitative expansion of abstract labor (205, 302)—and shows how crucial it has been to modernity and capitalism.

26. For a striking example of the axiomatization of matter, see William Cronon's account (1991, chapter 3) of the transformation of wheat into an equalized, homogenized, compared content.

27. Compared to craft know-how, which is situated or context specific, scientific knowledge of intensive properties is axiomatic (or "universal")—abstract and able to be inserted into widely different of production processes.

28. As Deleuze and Guattari put it, "Knowledge, information, and specialized education are just as much parts of capital ('knowledge capital') as is the most elementary labour of the worker" (1983, 234).

29. Deleuze and Guattari on the axiomatic nature of the modern legal system: "The law ceases to be the overcoding of customs, as it was in the archaic empire; it is no longer a set of topics, as it was in the evolved States, the autonomous cities, and the feudal systems; it increasingly assumes the direct form and immediate characteristics of an axiomatic, as evidenced in our civil 'code'" (1987, 453).

30. The axiomatization of human populations in denumerable sets is a key feature of what Foucault called "biopower" (1990, 2004a).

31. See also Roffe (2015), on which parts of this chapter draw. At one point (1987, 473), Deleuze and Guattari use the expression "non-denumerable aggregates," which would have prevented the confusion had they always used it instead of "non-denumerable sets."

32. Such a mode of belonging is a key feature of Deleuze and Guattari's concept of the rhizome (1987, Plateau 1). Roffe says about their use of set theory that "the crucial problem is that there is no possible distinction in kind . . . between different ways of belonging, between (for example) connection and conjunction. For set theory, it is strictly size that matters and nothing else" (2016, 146).

33. Deleuze and Guattari clarify the difference between conjugation and connection this way:

> At this point, we must introduce a distinction between the two notions of connection and conjugation of flows. "Connection" indicates the way in which decoded and deterritorialized flows boost one another, accelerate their shared escape, and augment or stoke their quanta; the "conjugation" of these same flows, on the other hand, indicates their relative stoppage, like a point of accumulation that plugs or seals the lines of flight, performs a general reterritorialization, and brings the flows under the dominance of a single flow capable of overcoding them. (1987, 220)

34. Following Nietzsche, and going against the grain of some Marxisms, Deleuze and Guattari insist,

> Libidinal investment does not bear upon the regime of the social syntheses, but upon the degree of development of the forces or the energies on which these syntheses depend. . . . It does not bear upon the social means and ends, but upon . . . the form of power for itself, devoid of meaning and purpose, since the meanings and the purposes derive from it, and not the contrary. . . . To be sure, the role, the place, and the part one has in a society, and from which one inherits in terms of the

laws of social reproduction, impel the libido to invest a given socius as a full body—a given absurd power in which we participate, or have the chance to participate, under the cover of aims and interests. The fact remains that there exists a disinterested love of the social machine, of the form of power, and of the degree of development in and for themselves. (1983, 345–46)

35. On the distinction between power with and power over, see Holland (2011, 67–72). The distinction is akin to a distinction drawn in recent French thought between the terms *puissance* and *pouvoir*, based in large part on Anthony Negri's reading of *potentia* and *potestas* in Spinoza (Negri, 1991; see also Casarino and Negri 2008). Anglo-American political philosophy makes a similar (though not identical) distinction between freedom to and freedom from (or positive and negative freedom). In connection with markets, the corresponding terms are the social division of labor (power with) and the political division of labor (power over).

36. Deleuze and Guattari explain that "minorities do not receive a better solution of their problem by integration, even with axioms, statutes, autonomies, independences. Their tactics necessarily go that route. But if they are revolutionary, it is because they carry within them a deeper movement that challenges the worldwide axiomatic" (1987, 472).

37. Deleuze and Guattari adopt the thesis of the revolutionary self-abolition of the proletariat from Mario Tronti (187, 571–2, n. 67): "As long as the working class defines itself by an acquired status, or even by a theoretically conquered State, it appears only as 'capital,' a part of capital (variable capital), and does not leave the plan(e) of capital. At best, the plan(e) becomes bureaucratic. On the other hand, it is by leaving the plan(e) of capital, and never ceasing to leave it, that a mass becomes increasingly revolutionary and destroys the dominant equilibrium of the denumerable sets" (187, 472). For a comprehensive treatment of Deleuze and Guattari's debts to Marx, and to Italian Marxism in particular, see Thoburn (2003).

38. For a detailed program to rescue power with from power over, drawing on both normative philosophy and empirical social science (albeit while explicitly sidestepping the obstacles of capitalism and class), see Allen and Somanathan (2020).

Conclusion

1. In its transformation of psychoanalysis, the difference of regime highlighted in schizoanalysis involves only the separation of the family from the capitalist economy. Modernity, however, is known for also separating the sphere of politics from the domestic sphere and the economy. But in the case of Charles Baudelaire, as I have shown (1993), despite the modern separation of life into these distinct spheres, his personal, political and economic circumstances resonated with one another: the

loss of his paternal inheritance to the stepfather his mother married threw him onto the market as a seller rather than the consummate consumer dandy he had been in his youth, just as the defeat of Revolution of 1848 by the authoritarian Second Empire of Napoleon III dashed the romantic-socialist hopes he shared with so many of his generation—making him the premier poet of modernity, or in Benjamin's phrase (1973), the "lyric poet in the era of high capitalism."

2. I include in the meaning of "postmodern" the sense that we know that modernity hasn't turned out as expected, but we don't know exactly what social formation will replace it or what it will be called. More often than "a new axiomatic" (1987, 471) Deleuze and Guattari speak of "a new earth and a new people" (1994, 99–101) or a "people to come" (1994, 109) summoned by utopian philosophy to follow and replace "civilized society" (i.e., capitalism). But see Latour's detailed program to explore the question of whether there is "another system of coordinates that can replace the one we have lost, now that the modernist parenthesis is closing" (2103, 10); and Vanessa Machado de Oliveira's equally detailed program for "hospicing modernity" (2021). Machado quite rightly suggests (2021, 91) that "modernity" should really be called "modernity/coloniality," identifying colonialism as "the constitutive underside of modernity: inherently extractive, relationally unethical, and ecologically unsustainable," but examining the considerable overlap between the cultural mindset and practices she calls "coloniality" (which includes but is far broader than colonialism itself) and the diagnosis of Sadism presented here lies well beyond the scope of this book.

3. The Trump cult of personality can be considered a personification of capitalism in the sense that Walter Benjamin (2004, 259) has suggested that capitalism is not merely a "religiously conditioned construction, as Weber thought," but an "essentially religious phenomenon. . . . a pure religious cult." This, he argues, is because it "knows no special dogma, no theology"—in other words, because it has sacrificed ends (qualitative values, whether theological or not) to means (growth). Not all religions can be considered cults, but there is a cult aspect to all religions: belonging to the group counts for at least as much as the content of what the group supposedly stands for or advocates. Hence the patently absurd content of many religions—for example, virgin birth of the deity—which must be taken as an article of cult-faith (or *point de capiton*) to secure the sense of belonging. The Trump candidacy is a cult of personality in this precise sense: it has no coherent policy content; what matters is belonging to the group and sharing vicariously (via superego identification) in the power accruing to the leader of the group. Hence his boast that he could shoot someone on Fifth Avenue and not suffer any loss of popularity. As in Machiavelli's analysis of the prince and Nietzsche's analysis of the priest, raw power arises from assembling bodies and souls into a group or herd, without requiring a commitment to doing any good.

4. See Graeber (2011, especially chapter 10) and Braudel (1979), who goes so far as to call capitalist markets "anti-markets."

5. In fact, capitalists have from the start "all[ied] themselves with political authorities to limit the freedom of the market," establish "some kind of formal or de facto monopoly" (Graeber 2011, 260), and thereby act as price makers.

6. For similar accounts of the relation between capitalism and the death instinct, see Dostaler and Maris (2009) and Fong (2016).

7. See Marcuse (1964, chapter 3, especially 72–79), where it is also called "administered," "institutionalized," and "controlled" desublimation.

8. The privatized nature of Masochistic consumerism under capitalism contributes significantly to the crisis; Mike Davis even goes so far as to suggest that "there is no planetary shortage of 'carrying capacity' if we are willing to make democratic public space, rather than modular, private consumption, the engine of sustainable equality. Public affluence—represented by great urban parks, free museums, libraries, and infinite possibilities for human interaction—represents an alternative route to a rich standard of life based on Earth-friendly sociality" (2018, 218).

9. On markets themselves as a potential platform for formulating the common good, see Holland (2011, especially chapter 4). For an argument suggesting politics could serve as such a platform, see Badiou (2014).

10. The two concepts come from two very different theoretical perspectives (notably regarding the concept of repression), but they are addressing the same aspect of advanced capitalist society.

11. I have explored the positive potential of capital-free markets in my book *Nomad Citizenship* (2011).

12. For a contrasting perspective on the environment's survival prospects under capitalism, see Stanford University's "Natural Capital Project" (https://naturalcapitalproject.stanford.edu/), which operates on the premise that accounting for the "natural" value of the environment by factoring it as a cost of production into surplus-value calculations—that is, axiomatizing nature—is compatible with capital-compelled growth ad infinitum. But see Moore (2015) for reasons why this gamble is unlikely to pay off as the centuries-old regime of what he calls "Cheap Nature" reaches its end. But factoring environmental costs into profit calculations might make it apparent that capitalism is unsustainable economically as well as environmentally.

13. On the effects of widespread precarity on mental health more generally, see Fisher (2009, 2014).

14. If the temporal dynamics of capitalism can be considered Masochistic because of the role that suspense and deferral play, its spatial dynamics can be considered Sadistic, in its striation of space by latitude and longitude, surveying, and cartography in the service of private property, colonialism, and the location and exploitation of natural resources.

15. In examining the historical evolution of Deleuze and Guattai's thought—including Deleuze's "Postscript on the Societies of Control" (1992)—in the context of neoliberalism, Schleusener (2020, 46) describes this shift from fixity to

continual self-modification thusly: "Under the conditions of global capitalism, mobility . . . seems to have lost its cultural value as a means to escape from repressive social assemblages and overstep rigid boundaries, since mobility itself has become the general rule to which almost anyone now has to conform."

16. That dynamic was crucial to Trump's takeover of the Republican Party and rise to power starting with his successful 2016 presidential election campaign.

17. On resonance as a key component of operations of capture, see Deleuze and Guattari (1987, particularly plateau 13); see also Connolly (2008) for a similar characterization of what he calls the "evangelical-capitalist resonance machine."

Works Cited

Abend, S. M., M. S. Porder, et al. 1983. *Borderline Patients: Psychoanalytic Perspectives*. New York: International Universities Press.
Adorno, T. W. 1950. *The Authoritarian Personality*. New York: Harper.
Adorno, T. W. 1967–68. "Sociology and Psychology." *New Left Review* 46–47: 63–80, 79–97.
Adorno, Theodor. 2016. "Remarks on *The Authoritarian Personality*." *The Platypus Affiliated Society*, November. Accessed May 18, 2023. https://platypus1917.org/2016/11/08/remarks-authoritarian-personality-adorno-frenkel-brunswik-levinson-sanford/.
Allen, D., and R. Somanathan. 2020. *Difference without Domination: Pursuing Justice in Diverse Democracies*. Chicago: University of Chicago Press.
Altemeyer, B. 1996. *The Authoritarian Specter*. Cambridge: Harvard University Press.
Althusser, L. 2006. *Philosophy of the Encounter: Later Writings, 1978–87*. London: Verso.
Andreas-Salomé, L. 1990. *Fenitschka and Deviations: Two Novellas*. Lanham: University Press of America.
Ansell-Pearson, K., ed. 1997. *Deleuze and Philosophy: The Difference Engineer*. London: Routledge.
Arbuthnot, J. 1773. *An Inquiry into The Connection Between the Present Price of Provisions, and the Size of Farms*. London: T. Cadell.
Bacon, F. 2000. *The Advancement of Learning*. Oxford: Clarendon.
Bacon, F. 2002. *Valerius Terminus; of the Interpretation of Nature*. R. L. Ellis and G. Engel, Project Gutenberg.
Badiou, A. 2014. *For a Politics of the Common Good*. New York: Columbia University Press.
Bakhtin, M. 1968. *Rabelais and His World*. Cambridge, MA: MIT Press.
Barker, Tim. 2019. "Other People's Blood." N+1, February. https://www.nplusonemag.com/online-only/online-only/other-peoples-blood/.
Bataille, G. 1988. *The Accursed Share: An Essay on General Economy*. New York: Zone Books.
Bateson, G. 1972. *Steps to an Ecology of Mind*. New York: Ballantine Books.

Battan, J. F. 1983. "The "New Narcissism" in 20th-Century America: The Shadow and Substance of Social Change." *Journal of Social History* 172: 199–220.
Baumeister, R. F. 1989. *Masochism and the Self.* Hillsdale, NJ: Lawrence Erlbaum Associates.
Beckman, F. 2013. *Between Desire and Pleasure: A Deleuzian Theory of Sexuality.* Edinburgh: Edinburgh University Press.
Benjamin, W. 1969. *Illuminations.* New York: Schocken Books.
Benjamin, W. 1973. *Charles Baudelaire: A Lyric Poet in the Era of High Capitalism.* London: New Left Books.
Benjamin, W. 2004. "Capitalism as Religion." In *The Frankfurt School on Religion: Key Writings by the Major Thinkers*, edited by E. Medieta, 259–62. New York: Routledge.
Bensaïd, Daniel. 2014. *The Dispossessed.* Minneapolis: University of Minnesota Press
Bersani, L., and A. Phillips 2008. *Intimacies.* Chicago: University of Chicago Press.
Braudel, F. 1979. *Civilization and Capitalism, 15th–18th Century.* New York: Harper & Row.
Brown, N. O. 1959. *Life against Death: The Psychoanalytical Meaning of History.* Middletown, CT: Wesleyan University Press.
Brown, W. 1995. *States of Injury: Power and Freedom in Late Modernity.* Princeton, NJ: Princeton University Press.
Brown, W. 2015. *Undoing the Demos: Neoliberalism's Stealth Revolution.* Cambridge: MIT Press.
Brunhoff, S. d. 1971. *L'offre de monnaie (critique d'un concept).* Paris: F. Maspero.
Bryant, L. R. 2008. *Difference and Givenness: Deleuze's Transcendental Empiricism and the Ontology of Immanence.* Evanston, IL: Northwestern University Press.
Buchen, L. 2009. "Schizophrenic Brain Not Fooled by Optical Illusion." *Wired,* April. https://www.wired.com/2009/04/schizoillusion/.
Campbell, C. 1987. *The Romantic Ethic and the Spirit of Modern Consumerism.* Oxford: Blackwell.
Camus, A. 1989. *The Stranger.* New York: Vintage International.
Casarino, C., and A. Negri. 2008. *In Praise of the Common.* Minneapolis: University of Minnesota Press
Casilli, A. 1996. *La fabbrica libertina: De Sade e il sistema industriale.* Roma: Manifestolibri.
Chalmers, D. M. 1987. *Hooded Americanism: The History of the Ku Klux Klan.* Durham: Duke University Press.
Chien, Y.-L., M. H. Hsieh, et al. 2019. "P50-N100-P200 Sensory Gating Deficits in Adolescents and Young Adults with Autism Spectrum Disorders." *Progress in Neuro-Psychopharmacology and Biological Psychiatry* 95. DOI: https://doi.org/10.1016/j.pnpbp.2019.109683
Clecak, P. 1983. *America's Quest for the Ideal Self: Dissent and Fulfillment in the 60s and 70s.* New York: Oxford University Press.

Connolly, W. E. 2008. *Capitalism and Christianity: American Style*. Durham: Duke University Press.
Cooper, M. 2008. *Life as Surplus: Biotechnology and Capitalism in the Neoliberal Era*. Seattle: University of Washington Press.
Crasta, J. E., W. J. Gavin, et al. 2021. "Expanding Our Understanding of Sensory Gating in Children with Autism Spectrum Disorders." *Clinical Neurophysiology* 132 (1): 180–90.
Cronon, W. 1991. *Nature's Metropolis: Chicago and the Great West*. New York: W. W. Norton.
Crosby, A. 1997. *The Measure of Reality*. Cambridge: Cambridge University Press.
Davis, M. 2018. *Old Gods, New Enigmas: Marx's Lost Theory*. London: Verso.
Deleuze, G. 1986. *Cinema 1: The Movement-Image*. Minneapolis: University of Minnesota Press.
Deleuze, G. 1988. *Bergsonism*. New York: Zone Books.
Deleuze, G. 1989. *Cinema 2: The Time-Image*. Minneapolis: University of Minnesota Press.
Deleuze, G. 1990. *The Logic of Sense*. New York: Columbia University Press.
Deleuze, G. 1992. "Postscript on the Societies of Control." In *Negotiations*, 177–82. New York: Columbia University Press.
Deleuze, G. 1994. *Difference and Repetition*. New York: Columbia University Press.
Deleuze, G. 1997. *Essays Critical and Clinical*. Minneapolis: University of Minnesota Press.
Deleuze, G. 2004. *Francis Bacon: The Logic of Sensation*. Minneapolis: University of Minnesota Press.
Deleuze, G., and F. Guattari. 1983. *Anti-Oedipus: Capitalism and Schizophrenia*. Minneapolis: University of Minnesota Press.
Deleuze, G., and F. Guattari. 1987. *A Thousand Plateaus: Capitalism and Schizophrenia*. Minneapolis: University of Minnesota Press.
Deleuze, G., and F. Guattari. 1994. *What Is Philosophy?* New York: Columbia University Press.
Deleuze, G., and C. Parnet. 2011. *Gilles Deleuze from A to Z*. Semiotext(e) foreign agents series. Cambridge, MA: MIT Press: 3 videodiscs (331 min.).
Deleuze, G. 1971. *Masochism: An Interpretation of Coldness and Cruelty*, together with the entire text of *Venus in Furs*. New York: G. Braziller.
Descartes, R. 2006. *A Discourse on the Method of Correctly Conducting One's Reason and Seeking Truth in the Sciences*. Oxford: Oxford University Press.
Di Muzio, T., and R. H. Robbins. 2016. *Debt as Power*. Manchester, UK: Manchester University Press.
Dick, M.-D., and R. McLaughlan. 2020. *Late Capitalist Freud in Literary, Cultural, and Political Theory*. Cham, Switzerland: Palgrave Macmillan.
Dostaler, G., and B. Maris 2009. *Capitalisme et pulsion de mort*. Paris: Albin Michel.

Elliott, R. C. 1972. *The Power of Satire: Magic, Ritual, Art*. Princeton: Princeton University Press.
Ellis, B. E. 1991. *American Psycho: A Novel*. New York: Vintage Books.
Fink, B. 1995. *The Lacanian Subject: Between Language and Jouissance*. Princeton, NJ: Princeton University Press.
Finn, D. K. 2006. *The Moral Ecology of Markets: Assessing Claims about Markets and Justice*. Cambridge: Cambridge University Press.
Fisher, Mark. 2009. *Capitalist Realism: Is There No Alternative?* Winchester: Zero Books.
Fisher, Mark. 2014. *Ghosts of My Life: Writings on Depression, Hauntology and Lost Futures*. Winchester: Zero Books.
Fong, B. Y. 2016. *Death and Mastery: Psychoanalytic Drive Theory and the Subject of Late Capitalism*. New York: Columbia University Press.
Foucault, M. 1977. *Language, Counter-Memory, Practice: Selected Essays and Interviews*. Ithaca, NY: Cornell University Press.
Foucault, M. 1979. *Discipline and Punish: The Birth of the Prison*. New York: Vintage/Random House.
Foucault, M. 1990. *The History of Sexuality: An Introduction*. London: Penguin.
Foucault, M. 2004a. *"Society Must Be Defended": Lectures at the Collège de France, 1975–76*. London: Penguin Books.
Foucault, M. 2004b. *The Birth of Biopolitics: Lectures at the Collège de France, 1978–79*. New York: Picador.
French, David. 2023. "The Rage and Joy of MAGA America." *New York Times*, July 8, 2023, sec. Opinion.
Freud, S. 1953. *Beyond the Pleasure Principle. Standard Edition of the Complete Psychological Works of Sigmund Freud*. London: Hogarth. 18:3–64.
Freud, S. 1953. *Civilization and Its Discontents. Standard Edition of the Complete Psychological Works of Sigmund Freud*. London: Hogarth. 21:57–145.
Freud, S. 1953. *The Ego and the Id. Standard Edition of the Complete Psychological Works of Sigmund Freud*. London: Hogarth. 19:3–66.
Freud, S. 1953. *Future of an Illusion. Standard Edition of the Complete Psychological Works of Sigmund Freud*. London: Hogarth. 21:5–56.
Freud, S. 1953. *The Interpretation of Dreams. Standard Edition of the Complete Psychological Works of Sigmund Freud*. London: Hogarth. 4: xxiii–338, 5:339–621.
Freud, S. 1953. *Moses and Monotheism. Standard Edition of the Complete Psychological Works of Sigmund Freud*. London: Hogarth. 23:7–138.
Freud, S. 1953. *On Narcissism. Standard Edition of the Complete Psychological Works of Sigmund Freud*. London: Hogarth. 14:67–102.
Freud, S. 1953. *An Outline of Psychoanalysis. Standard Edition of the Complete Psychological Works of Sigmund Freud*. London: Hogarth. 23:139–208.
Freud, S. 1953. *Project for a Scientific Psychology. Standard Edition of the Complete Psychological Works of Sigmund Freud*. London: Hogarth. 1:283–397.

Freud, S. 1953. *Remembering, Repeating, and Working-Through. Standard Edition of the Complete Psychological Works of Sigmund Freud.* London: Hogarth. 12:147–56.
Freud, S. 1953. *Standard Edition of the Complete Psychological Works of Sigmund Freud.* London: Hogarth.
Freud, S. 1953. *Three Essays on the Theory of Sexuality. Standard Edition of the Complete Psychological Works of Sigmund Freud.* London: Hogarth. 7:130–243.
Freud, S. 1953. *Totem and Taboo. Standard Edition of the Complete Psychological Works of Sigmund Freud.* London: Hogarth. 13:1–240.
Fromm, E. 1976. *Escape from Freedom.* New York: Holt, Rinehart and Winston.
Gilder, G. F. 1981. *Wealth and Poverty.* New York: Basic Books.
Girard, R. 1965. *Deceit, Desire, and the Novel: Self and Other in Literary Structure.* Baltimore: Johns Hopkins University.
Glick, R. A., and D. I. Meyers 1988. *Masochism: Current Psychoanalytic Perspectives.* Hillsdale, NJ: Analytic.
Goffman, E. 1959. *The Presentation of Self in Everyday Life.* Garden City, NY: Doubleday.
Goldmann, L. 1975. *Towards a Sociology of the Novel.* London: Tavistock.
Graeber, D. 2011. *Debt: The First 5,000 Years.* Brooklyn, NY: Melville House.
Graeber, D. 2019. *Bullshit Jobs.* New York: Simon and Schuster.
Hahn, B., B. M. Robinson, et al. 2022. "Impaired Filtering and Hyperfocusing: Neural Evidence for Distinct Selective Attention Abnormalities in People with Schizophrenia." *Cerebral Cortex* 9 (1): 1950–1964.
Haney, C., C. Banks, et al. 1973. "Interpersonal Dynamics in a Simulated Prison." *International Journal of Criminology and Penology* 1 (1): 69–97.
Hanly, M. A. F. 1995. *Essential Papers on Masochism.* New York: New York University Press.
Hardt, M., and A. Negri. 2009. *Commonwealth.* Cambridge: Harvard University Press.
Harvey, D. 2005a. *A Brief History of Neoliberalism.* New York: Oxford University Press.
Harvey, D. 2005b. *The New Imperialism.* Oxford: Oxford University Press.
Heise, U. K. 1997. *Chronoschisms: Time, Narrative, and Postmodernism.* Cambridge: Cambridge University Press.
Henrich, J. P. 2020. *The WEIRDest People in the World: How the West Became Psychologically Peculiar and Particularly Prosperous.* New York: Farrar, Straus and Giroux.
Hobsbawm, E. J. 1975. *The Age of Capital, 1848–1875.* New York: Scribner.
Hofstadter, R. 1965. *The Paranoid Style in American Politics, and Other Essays.* New York: Knopf.
Holland, E. W. 1993. *Baudelaire and Schizoanalysis: The Sociopoetics of Modernism.* Cambridge: Cambridge University Press.
Holland, E. W. 1999. *Deleuze and Guattari's "Anti-Oedipus": Introduction to Schizoanalysis.* London: Routledge.

Holland, E. W. 2011. *Nomad Citizenship: Free-Market Communism and the Slow-Motion General Strike*. Minneapolis: University of Minnesota Press.

Horkheimer, M., and T. W. Adorno 1972. *Dialectic of Enlightenment*. New York: Herder and Herder.

Jacoby, R. 1983. *The Repression of Psychoanalysis: Otto Fenichel and the Political Freudians*. New York: Basic Books.

Jameson, F. 1991. *Postmodernism, or, The Cultural Logic of Late Capitalism*. Durham: Duke University Press.

Jarvis, C. 2016. *Exquisite Masochism: Marriage, Sex, and the Novel Form*. Baltimore: Johns Hopkins University Press.

Jewison, Norman, dir. 1975. *Rollerball*. Metro-Goldwyn-Mayer.

Jones, E. 1960. *The Life and Work of Sigmund Freud*. New York: Basic Books.

Kant, I. 2007. *Critique of Judgement*. Oxford: Oxford University Press.

Karatani, K. J. 2003. *Transcritique on Kant and Marx*. Cambridge, MA: MIT Press.

Kelton, S. 2020. *The Deficit Myth: Modern Monetary Theory and the Birth of the People's Economy*. New York: Hachette Book Group.

Kernberg, O. F. 1975. *Borderline Conditions and Pathological Narcissism*. New York: Aronson.

Klas, D., and W. Offenkranz 1976. "Sartre's Contribution to the Understanding of Narcissism." *International Journal of Psychoanalytic Psychotherapy* 5:547–65.

Klein, N. 2019. *On Fire: the (Burning) Case for a Green New Deal*. New York: Simon & Schuster.

Kohut, H. 1971. *The Analysis of the Self: A Systematic Approach to the Psychoanalytic Treatment of Narcissistic Personality Disorders*. New York: International Universities Press.

Kordela, K. 2023. "Marx's Affect." *Cultural Critique* 120:43–60.

Kornbluh, A. 2014. *Realizing Capital: Financial and Psychic Economies in Victorian Form*. New York: Fordham University Press.

Kornbluh, A. 2017. "We Have Never Been Critical: Toward the Novel as Critique." *Novel: A Forum on Fiction* 50 (3): 397–408.

Kornbluh, A. 2019. *The Order of Forms: Realism, Formalism, and Social Space*. Chicago: University of Chicago Press.

Kucich, J. 2007. *Imperial Masochism: British Fiction, Fantasy, and Social Class*. Princeton: Princeton University Press.

Lacan, J. 1977. *The Four Fundamental Concepts of Psychoanalysis*. London: Hogarth.

Lacan, J. 1989. "Kant with Sade." *October* 51: 55–75.

Lacan, J. 1998. *On Feminine Sexuality: The Limits of Love and Knowledge*, book 10. *Encore 1972–1973*. New York: W. W. Norton.

Lacan, J. 2006. *Ecrits: The First Complete Edition in English*. New York: W. W. Norton.

Lacan, J. 2007. *The Seminar of Jacques Lacan*. Book 17, *The Other Side of Psychoanalysis: 1969–1970*. New York: Norton.

Lasch, C. 1978. *The Culture of Narcissism: American Life in an Age of Diminishing Expectations*. New York: W.W. Norton.

Lasch, C. 1984. *The Minimal Self: Psychic Survival in Troubled Times.* New York: W. W. Norton.
Latour, Bruno. 1993. *We Have Never Been Modern.* Cambridge, MA: Harvard University Press.
Latour, Bruno. 2013. *An Inquiry into Modes of Existence: An Anthropology of the Moderns.* Cambridge, MA: Harvard University Press.
Lautman, A. 1938. *Essai sur l'unité des sciences mathématiques dans leur développement actuel.* Paris: Hermann & cie.
Lazzarato, M. 2012. *The Making of the Indebted Man: An Essay on the Neoliberal Condition.* Los Angeles: Semiotext(e).
Lazzarato, M. 2015. *Governing by Debt.* Cambridge MA: MIT Press.
Lee, Bandy X, ed. 2019. *The Dangerous Case of Donald Trump: 37 Psychiatrists and Mental Health Experts Assess a President.* Updated and expanded second edition. New York: Thomas Dunne Books: St. Martin's.
Lesjak, C. 2006. *Working Fictions: A Genealogy of the Victorian Novel.* Durhman, NC: Duke University Press.
Levine, C. 2003. *The Serious Pleasures of Suspense: Victorian Realism and Narrative Doubt.* Charlottesville: University of Virginia Press.
Luck, S. J., C. J. Leonard, et al. 2019. "Is Attentional Filtering Impaired in Schizophrenia?" *Schizophrenia Bulletin* 45 (5): 1001–11.
Lukács, G. 1971a. "Reification and the Consciousness of the Proletariat." *History and Class Consciousness.* Cambridge, MA: MIT Press, 83–222.
Lukács, G. 1971b. *Writer & Critic, and Other Essays.* New York: Grosset & Dunlap.
Luther, M. 2017. *The Ninety-Five Theses and Other Writings.* New York: Penguin Books.
Lynch, D. 1998. *The Economy of Character: Novels, Market Culture, and the Business of Inner Meaning.* Chicago: University of Chicago Press.
Lyotard, J.-F. 1984. *The Postmodern Condition: A Report on Knowledge.* Minneapolis: University of Minnesota Press.
Lysack, K. 2008. *Come Buy, Come Buy: Shopping and the Culture of Consumption in Victorian Women's Writing.* Athens: Ohio University Press.
Machado de Oliveira, V. 2021. *Hospicing Modernity: Facing Humanity's Wrongs and the Implications for Social Activism.* Berkeley: North Atlantic Books.
Machiavelli, N. 1968. *The Prince.* Oxford: Oxford University Press.
Mader, M. B. 2017. "Philosophical and Scientific Intensity in the Thought of Gilles Deleuze." *Deleuze Studies* 11 (2): 259–77.
Malcolm, H. 1971. *Generation of Narcissus.* Boston: Little, Brown.
Mallarme, S. 2012. *La Musique et les lettres.* Paris: Hacehette.
Manning, E. 2016. *The Minor Gesture.* Durham: Duke University Press.
Marcuse, H. 1955. *Eros and Civilization: A Philosophical Inquiry into Freud.* Boston: Beacon.
Marcuse, H. 1964. *One-dimensional Man: Studies in the Ideology of Advanced Industrial Society.* Boston: Beacon.

Marin, Peter. 1975. "The New Narcissism." *Harper's*, October 1, 45. https://www.proquest.com/magazines/new-narcissism/docview/1301540034/se-2.

Marx, K., and F. Engels. 1975. *Collected Works*, volume 28. *Grundrisse: Foundations of the Critique of Political Economy*. New York: International.

Marx, K., and F. Engels. 1975. *Collected Works*, volume 35. *Capital: A Critique of Political Economy*, volume 1. New York: International.

Marx, K., and F. Engels 1975. *Collected Works*, volume 37. *Capital: a Critique of Political Economy*, volume 3. New York: International.

Marx, Karl, and Friedrich Engels. 1969. *Karl Marx and Frederick Engels: Selected Works*. Moscow: Progress.

Massé, M. A. 1992. *In the Name of Love: Women, Masochism, and the Gothic*. Ithaca: Cornell University Press.

Mauss, M. 2002. *The Gift: Forms and Functions of Exchange in Archaic Societies*. London: Routledge.

McGowan, T. 2004. *The End of Dissatisfaction? Jacques Lacan and the Emerging Enjoyment Society*. Albany: SUNY Press.

McGowan, T. 2016. *Capitalism and Desire: The Psychic Cost of Free Markets*. New York: Columbia University Press.

Melloan, G. 2003. "Some Reflections on My 32 Years with Bartley." *Wall Street Journal*. New York.

Mennel, B. 2001. "Leopold Von Sacher-Masoch's 'Ein Weiblicher Sultan: Historischer Roman in Drei Teilen' (1873): Public Sadism/Private Masochism." *Modern Austrian Literature* 34 (1–2): 1–14.

Moore, J. 2015. *Capitalism in the Web of Life: Ecology and the Accumulation of Capital*. New York: Verso.

Moore, J. 2023. "Kapitalismus, Natur und der prometheische Blick von Mercator bis zum Weltraumzeitalter." In *Image Ecology*, edited by K. Schönegg and B. Levin. Leipzig: Spector Books.

More, T. 2002. *Utopia*. Cambridge: Cambridge University Press.

Mumford, L. 1967. *The Myth of the Machine*. New York: Harcourt.

Nakajima, M., L. I. Schmitt, et al. 2019. "Prefrontal Cortex Regulates Sensory Filtering through a Basal Ganglia-to-Thalamus Pathway." *Neuron* 103 (3): 445–58.

Negri, A. 1991. *The Savage Anomaly: The Power of Spinoza's Metaphysics and Politics*. Minneapolis: University of Minnesota Press.

Nitzan, J., and S. Bichler 2009. *Capital as Power: A Study of Order and Creorder*. New York: Routledge.

Noble, M. 2000. *The Masochistic Pleasures of Sentimental Literature*. Princeton, NJ: Princeton University Press.

Noyes, J. K. 1997. *The Mastery of Submission: Inventions of Masochism*. Ithaca, NY: Cornell University Press.

Oppel, R., Jr. 2004. "Energy Hogs: Enron Traders on Grandma Millie and Making Out Like Bandits." *New York Times*, June 13, 2004, sec. "Week in Review."

Patel, Raj. 2010. *The Value of Nothing*. New York: Picador.
Pateman, C. 1988. *The Sexual Contract*. Stanford, CA: Stanford University Press.
Patton, P. 2000. *Deleuze and the Political*. London, Routledge.
Penney, J. 2006. *The World of Perversion: Psychoanalysis and the Impossible Absolute of Desire*. Albany: SUNY Press.
Perec, G. 1990. *Things: A Story of the Sixties*. Boston: David Godine.
Perelman, M. 2000. *The Invention of Capitalism: Classical Political Economy and the Secret History of Primitive Accumulation*. Durham, NC: Duke University Press.
Perelman, M. 2013. "A Short History of Primitive Accumulation." *Counterpunch*, April. https://www.counterpunch.org/2013/04/16/a-short-history-of-primitive-accumulation/.
Pistor, K. 2019. *The Code of Capital: How the Law Creates Wealth and Inequality*. Princeton: Princeton University Press.
Polanyi, K. 1944. *The Great Transformation*. New York: Farrar & Rinehart.
Poovey, M. 2008. *Genres of the Credit Economy: Mediating Value in Eighteenth- and Nineteenth-Century Britain*. Chicago: University of Chicago Press.
Poster, M. 1978. *Critical Theory of the Family*. London: Pluto.
Postone, M. 1993. *Time, Labor, and Social Domination: A Reinterpretation of Marx's Critical Theory*. Cambridge: Cambridge University Press.
Price, C. C., and K. A. Edwards 2020. "Trends in Income From 1975 to 2018." DOI: https://www.rand.org/pubs/working_papers/WRA516-1.html.
Princen, Thomas. 2005. *The Logic of Sufficiency*. Cambridge: MIT Press.
Protevi, J. 2013. *Life, War, Earth: Deleuze and the Sciences*. Minneapolis: University of Minnesota Press.
Read, J. 2003. *The Micro-Politics of Capital: Marx and the Prehistory of the Present*. Albany: SUNY Press.
Reich, W. 2000. *The Mass Psychology of Fascism*. New York: Farrar, Straus & Giroux.
Reik, T. 1941. *Masochism in Modern Man*. New York, Toronto: Farrar & Rinehart.
Reix, J. 2023. "The Rise of the 'Sigma Male,' a New Kind of Toxic Masculinity: How Memes of a Fictional Serial Killer Turned into an Un-Ironic Personality and Lifestyle." *Vice*. https://www.vice.com/en/article/dy7bxq/sigma-male-toxic-masculinity
Roffe, J. 2015. *Abstract Market Theory*. London: Palgrave Macmillan.
Roffe, J. 2016. "Axiomatic Set Theory in the Work of Deleuze and Guattari: A Critique." *Parrhesia* 23:129–54.
Rotman, B. 1993. *Signifying Nothing: The Semiotics of Zero*. Stanford, CA: Stanford University Press.
Rotman, B. 2000. *Mathematics as Sign: Writing, Imagining, Counting*. Stanford, CA: Stanford University Press.
Russell, B. 1938. *Principles of Mathematics*. New York: W. W. Norton.
Sartre, J.-P. 1964. *Nausea*. New York: New Directions.
Schleusener, S. 2020. "Deleuze and Neoliberalism." *Coils of the Serpent*, 6:39–54.

Sennett, R. 1974. *The Fall of Public Man.* New York: Knopf.
Singh, M. 2023. "Texas Governor Signs Bill Rescinding Water Breaks as Deadly Heat Grips State." *The Guardian,* June 23, 2023.
Sohn-Rethel, A. 1978. *Intellectual and Manual Labour: A Critique of Epistemology. Critical Social Studies.* Atlantic Highlands, NJ: Humanities.
Somers-Hall, H. (2023). "Binding and Axiomatics: Deleuze and Guattari's Transcendental Account of Capitalism." *Continental Philosophy Review* (56): 619–38.
Srnicek, N. 2016. *Platform Capitalism.* Cambridge: Polity.
Stewart-Steinberg, S. 1998. *Sublime Surrender: Male Masochism at the Fin-de-Siècle.* Ithaca, NY: Cornell University Press.
Strozier, C. B. 1994. *Apocalypse: On the Psychology of Fundamentalism in America.* Boston: Beacon.
Sweezy, P. 1942. *The Theory of Capitalist Development.* New York: Monthly Review.
Theweleit, K. 1987. *Male Fantasies.* Minneapolis: University of Minnesota Press.
Thoburn, N. 2003. *Deleuze, Marx and Politics.* London: Routledge.
Thompson, E. P. 1963. *The Making of the English Working Class.* New York: Pantheon Books.
Thorsteinsson, V. 2016. "Diachronic Binding: The Novel Form and the Gendered Temporalities of Debt and Credit." Comparative Studies. PhD dissertation, Columbus, Ohio State University.
Tomšič, S. 2012. "Three Notes on Science and Psychoanalysis." *Filozofski vestnik* 33 (2): 127–44.
Tomšič, S. 2015. *The Capitalist Unconscious: Marx and Lacan.* London: Verso.
Tsing, A. L. 2015. *The Mushroom at the End of the World: On the Possibility of Life in Capitalist Ruins.* Princeton: Princeton University Press.
Veblen, T. 1899. *The Theory of the Leisure Class.* New York: Macmillan.
Veblen, T. 1904. *The Theory of Business Enterprise.* New York: C. Scribner's Sons.
Ward, J. 2022. *The Loop: How Technology Is Creating a World without Choices and How to Fight Back.* New York: Hachette Books.
Watson, J. 1999. *Literature and Material Culture from Balzac to Proust: The Collection and Consumption of Curiosities.* Cambridge: Cambridge University Press.
Weber, M. 1946. *From Max Weber: Essays in Sociology.* New York: Oxford University Press.
Weber, M. 1958. *The Protestant Ethic and the Spirit of Capitalism.* New York: C. Scribner's Sons.
Williams, R. H. 1982. *Dream Worlds: Mass Consumption in Late Nineteenth-Century France.* Berkeley: University of California Press.
Wittgenstein, L. 1953. *Philosophical Investigations.* New York: Macmillan.
Wolfe, T. 1976. "The 'Me' Decade and the Third Great Awakening." *New York. New York* 9:33–36.
Wright, R. 1940. *Native Son.* New York: Harper & Brothers.

Yalcinkaya, G. 2022. "Rise and Grind: How 'Sigma Males' Are Upturning the Internet." *DazedDigital*, January. https://www.dazeddigital.com/science-tech/article/55208/1/rise-and-grind-how-sigma-male-memes-are-upturning-the-man-o-sphere.

Zimbardo, P. 1973. "A Pirandellian Prison: The Mind Is a Formidable Jailer." *New York Times Magazine*. April 8, 1973, Section 6, pp. 36, 38, 48–50, 53, 60.

Žižek, S. 1999. "'You May!'—Slavoj Žižek Writes about the Post-Modern Superego." *London Review of Books*. London. 21.

Zuboff, S. 2019. *The Age of Surveillance Capitalism: The Fight for a Human Future at the New Frontier of Power*. New York: PublicAffairs.

Zupančič, A. 2006. "When Surplus Enjoyment Meets Surplus Value." In *Jacques Lacan and the Other Side of Psychoanalysis*, edited by J. Clemens and R. Grigg, 155–78. Durhman: Duke University Press.

Index

absurd, the, 34–39. *See also* existentialism
accumulation, 82, 83, 129n25, 134n33; differential, 93, 105; endless/infinite, 14, 18–19, 40, 71, 73, 76, 84, 95, 102, 113–115; precedence over enjoyment, 73–74, 76–77, 79, 84, 86, 113, 130n1; primitive, 8, 69, 77, 81. *See also* capital; surplus value
Adorno, Theodor, 14–15, 49, 108, 119n5, 123n7–9, 126n2
American Psycho. See Ellis, Brett
antiproduction, 83–84, 129n24, 130n30
après coup. See *nachträglich*
asceticism, 11, 20, 70, 79, 121n16, 121n19
austerity, 3, 21, 32, 53, 57, 113, 115, 130n27
autism, 2, 33, 35, 37–39, 43
axioms, 59–60, 71, 85–87, 104; in mathematics, 85–87; struggle over; 95–96, 102–103, 112; supplementary, 61, 91, 95, 97, 99–100, 103, 108, 112. *See also* axiomatic; axiomatization
axiomatic, 69, 89, 93, 97, 100–102; mathematical, 60, 85; new, 104– 105, 108, 112; open, x, 62, 86–87; philosophical, 61–62; political implications, 101–106, 112. *See also* axioms; axiomatization
axiomatization, 60, 62, 71, 74, 80, 87, 97, 104, 133n26; capitalist form of, 85, 104; of human populations, 99–101, 134n30. *See also* conjugation; denumerable/nondenumerable sets
anxiety, 74, 78, 128n15; separation-, 6–8, 68, 76–79, 113–114; castration-, 68–69
authoritarian personality. *See* Adorno, Theodor

Bacon, Francis, 15–16, 18, 98, 119n5
Bataille, Georges, 75, 83, 125n20, 130n30
Baudelaire, Charles, x, 3, 135n1
belief, 21, 80
Benjamin, Walter, 3, 39, 136n1, 136n3
borderline conditions, x, 2–3, 29, 31–43 passim, 57; narcissism, 43–47; supremacism, 47–53; and polymorphous narcissism, 53–54
Brown, Norman O., x, 1, 6–7, 54–57, 69, 80, 110, 112, 124n18, 124n20

Brown, Wendy, 21, 121n18, 121n20

Camus, Albert, 10, 35–38. *See also* existentialism
capital, 19, 61, 79, 82, 86, 104; effects on the market, ix–x, 1–2, 7, 25, 42, 53, 61–62, 65, 68, 84, 89–90, 93, 104, 113–115, 120n14; finance, 92–94, 113; power of, 19, 28–29, 76–77, 96, 106, 109–110, 112, 114; smooth/striated, 96; structure and dynamics of, 69–74, 87, 90–92, 95–97, 107, 114. *See also* accumulation
capitalism, ix–x, 1–2, 8, 32, 45, 59, 62, 68, 81, 84, 85, 93, 108, 116; advanced, 3–4, 60, 82, 123n3, 137n10; and death, 75–79; and the family, 69–74; consumption/consumerism; 2, 26–28, 114; mercantile, 4, 19, 89–91, 93, 132n9; post-industrial, 61, 89, 123n2, 125n5; production; 2, 18–22, 82, 111, 113–114. *See also* austerity; dispossession; markets
castration. *See* anxiety, castration
conjugation, 62, 97, 101–104, 134n33. *See also* axiomatization, connection
connection (of flows), 101–104, 134n32, 134n33
contract: labor, 18, 28, 81, 122n28, 131n8; Masochean, 14, 26–29, 114, 118n6; sexual, 24; social, 23, 27

death, 6–8, 54, 68, 71–76; instinct, x, 6, 55, 57, 60, 67–68, 74–75, 78–79
debt, 31, 50, 57, 70–71, 92, 94, 128n19; infinite, 71–73, 92–93, 97, 105, 113–115 passim
decoding, 59–60, 72–74, 80, 128n19; and freedom, 60, 65, 74, 105, 112; and schizophrenia, 128n22, 126n4. *See also* axiomatization; recoding
Deleuze, Gilles: *Bergsonism*, 128n21; *Cinema 1*, 77; *Cinema 2*, 125n7; *Difference and Repetition*, 78, 85, 130n2; *Essays Critical and Clinical*, 65, 117n3, 122n26, 126n10; *Francis Bacon: The Logic of Sensation*, 74; *The Logic of Sense*, 65; "Postscript on the Societies of Control," 123n3, 128n19, 137n15
Deleuze and Guattari: *Anti-Oedipus*, 61, 63, 92, 102, 105, 108, 117n1, 126n1, 126n3, 127n7; *A Thousand Plateaus*, 61, 85, 105, 117n1, 125n2; *What is Philosophy?*, 61–64, 95, 103, 106, 125n2, 125n8
denumerable/non-denumerable sets, 62, 100–105, 134n30, 134n31, 135n37
dependency: familial, 6–7, 77; market, 7–8, 71, 77–79. *See also* precarity; separation-anxiety
Despotism, 59, 70–73, 75–76, 83, 92, 95–96
Descartes, René, 15, 18, 113
diagnosis, 9, 38, 41, 113, 136n2; and literature, ix–x, 1–3, 31–35, 39, 44, 46, 64–65, 114, 122n21, 126n10; and philosophy, x, 64, 65; and psychology, 42–43, 47, 50; in Masoch, 19, 22, 26–27, 31; in Sade, 11, 19–20
Dialectic of Enlightenment. *See* Horkheimer, Max
difference, 53, 78, 85, 88, 90–91; -engines, 74, 104; in regime, 108, 135n1
disintegration, psychic. *See* borderline conditions
dispossession, 8, 42, 53, 69, 77. *See also* austerity; primitive accumulation

division: of labor, 2, 33, 56, 94, 135n35; of leisure, 33, 56, 94
domestic (private) sphere, 14, 23–29, 56, 67, 70, 114, 121n21, 135n1
domination, 5, 13; by capital, x, 92; of labor, 16; political, 7, 104, 131n8; sexual, 15, 114. *See also* power-over

Ellis, Brett, 46–47, 123n6
environmental crisis, 81, 84, 85, 92, 105, 112, 115, 137n12
existentialism, 35, 39, 43–45, 59, 79
exploitation, 5, 7, 82, 86, 123n1, 125n5, 137n14

family, x, 5, 42, 45, 49, 56, 84, 135n1; nuclear, 44, 62, 67–71, 73–74, 79–81, 108, 124n13, 127n6, 127n10
fascism, xi, 4, 21, 49
flows, 59, 62, 86–87, 96–97, 99, 101–102, 104–105, 127n10; surplus value of, 89–91, 132n10, 134n33
Foucaullt, Michel, 21, 72–73, 75, 82, 121n18, 128n18, 128n19, 134n30
fragmentation, psychic. *See* borderline conditions
Freikorps. *See* supremacism, Aryan
Freud, Sigmund: *Beyond the Pleasure Principle*, 78, 128n14; *Civilization and Its Discontents*, 54; *The Ego and the Id*, 128n14; *Future of an Illusion*, 54; *The Interpretation of Dreams*, 4; *Moses and Monotheism*, 4; *On Narcissism*, 54; *An Outline of Psychoanalysis*, 128n14; *Project for a Scientific Psychology*, 117n1; *Remembering, Repeating, and Working-Through*, 117n1; *Three Essays on the Theory of Sexuality*, 124n18; *Totem and Taboo*, 4

fundementalism. *See* supremacism, Christian

Galileo, 15, 113
Girard, René, 24–26

Hobbes, 23
Horkheimer, Max, 13–15, 108, 119n5

ideal ego, 27, 32, 54–57
identity (personal), 25–29, 74, 82, 95, 111, 114–116
imaginative hedonism, 25–26, 31–32, 56, 70, 82, 129n26
introjection, 4, 7, 67, 126n2
infinite, 6, 64, 107–109; debt, 71, 72–73, 92–92, 97, 105, 113, 115; mathematical, 18, 62, 100; subjective representation, 72–73

Jameson, Fredric, 34, 67
Jewison, Norman, 39–41

Kant, Immanuel, 13–15, 18, 22, 118n4, 120n15, 125n7, 127n7, 128n21
Kernberg, Otto, 41–43, 123n5, 124n13

labor power, 59, 61, 68, 77, 82, 98, 115; commodification of, 16, 90–91, 113; reproduction of, 19, 28, 90–91; sale of, 7–8, 16, 20, 89, 132n9
Lacan, Jacques, x, 34, 79–84, 111, 123n1, 124n17, 128n16, 128n21, 129n24, 130n29, 133n24
Latour, Bruno, 107–109, 136n2
law, 61, 100, 108, 118n6, 131n8, 134n29
libido: in psychoanalysis, 54, 68–69, 72, 78; in schizoanaysis, 60, 68, 73, 126n2, 135n34

Locke, John, 15, 18, 113
Lukács, György, 39, 77
Luther, Martin, 11, 68–69, 83, 118n1

Machiavelli, Niccolo, 11–14, 136n3
Madame Bovary (Flaubert), 26, 29, 31, 57
Marcuse, Herbert, v, x, 1, 54, 82, 110–111, 124n16, 124n18, 137n7; administered society, 77, 112; performance principle, 5–7; primary narcissism, 54, polymorphous perversity, 57; surplus repression, 5–6, 82, 116
markets, 23, 27, 58, 59, 61, 69, 73–74, 78, 81, 107, 128n19; as multiplicity, 79, 87–88, 93–96, 105, 131n4; as universal; 61, 106, 112; capitalist, 89–92, 95–97; free/postcapitalist; x, 104–105, 109–112, 137n9, 137n11; job-, 8, 16, 28, 45, 49, 91, 130n27, 131n8; slope of, 92–93, 105, 115; world; 2, 33, 56, 61, 64, 95, 112. *See also* axiomatization
Marx, Karl, 21, 59, 60, 102, 118n8, 125n1, 126n2, 135n37; abstract labor, 86; finance capital, 92; primitive accumulation, 77; social power of money, 104
Masoch, Leopold von Sacher-, 22, 23, 32, 107, 117n1, 118n6; novels, x, 1–3 passim, 9, 14, 26–29 passim, 31, 41, 64, 117n3, 118n5, 121n21, 122n26, 126n10
Masochism, ix, 1–3, 8–9, 13–14, 32, 79, 107, 123n30, 133n21, 137n14; and capitalist consumerism, 26–29, 70, 76, 84, 95, 111, 114, 116, 118n7, 129n26, 130n27, 137n8
mathematics: and axiomatic (set) theory, 60, 62, 85–87, 97–99, 131n3; early modern, 15, 17–18, 20, 72, 113–114, 127n8
Mauss, Marcel, 75–76, 125n20
means of life, 8, 19–20, 42, 53, 60, 69–71, 75–77, 122n28, 123n2. *See also* austerity; dispossession
means/ends, 14, 76–79, 84, 102, 110, 114, 121n17, 136n3
minor/minority, 100–105. *See also* denumerable/non-denumerable sets
minorities, 23, 53, 100, 103, 123n9, 135n36
modernity, 4, 11–13, 25, 108–109, 131n5, 1333n25, 135n1, 136n2
money, 8, 19, 25, 31, 58, 95, 97, 104–105, 119n6, 119n7, 121n17; early modern, 16–18; circuits of, 40, 89–91, 96, 120n11, 131n8, 133n21; credit/debt, 91–94, 96, 132n13, 132n14
Moore, Jason, 18, 61, 91, 137n12; modernity, 107–108; real abstraction, 86, 133n25
More, Thomas, 11–12
multiplicity, 62, 74; minor, 100–101; world market as, 88, 91, 93–95, 106, 112, 131n4

narcissism, 2, 124n12, 124n13, 124n14, 124n15; borderline, x, 43–47, 57, 109, 123n5; polymorphous; 53–57, 60, 65, 102, 109, 114; primary, 54–56, 124n16; secondary, 54, 114
nachträglich/Nachträglichkeit, 1, 7, 42, 69, 78, 81–82, 110–111, 117n1
Native Son. *See* Wright, Richard
Nausea. *See under* Sartre, Jean-Paul
neoliberalism, 21–22, 49, 57, 109, 115, 121n18, 137n15

Nietzsche, Friedrich, 59, 65, 102, 125n1, 134n34, 136n3; on Kant, 13, 128n21
neurodiversity, 3, 57, 112, 114
neurosis, 4, 7, 42–43, 50, 55, 57, 78, 82, 104, 130n29; and perversion, 3, 8, 32, 41–42, 53, 78; and psychosis, 33, 41
Nuclear family. See under family

obedience, 21, 56, 70, 80
Oedipus complex, 44, 50, 54, 55; in psychoanalysis, 4, 68, 69, 72, 78, 80, 125n9; schizoanalytic critique of, x, 60, 67, 69–75, 127n6

paranoia, 41, 48–49, 60, 80, 102
partial objects, 55, 57, 124n17
Perec, Georges, 31–33
performance principle, 5–7, 57
perversion, ix–x, 1–2, 8, 19, 32, 76, 78, 113; of market dynamics, 84, 106, 110; vs. perversity, 57–58, 62, 65, 112–113, 115, 124n19. See also Sadism; Masochism
Perversity. See under perversion
postmodern, 33, 107–109, 136n2
power over/power with, 102, 104, 135n35, 135n38
precarity, 53, 57, 76–79, 109, 113–114, 137n13. See also dependency; separation-anxiety
privatization, 67, 69, 122n23
projection, 4, 7, 67, 72–73, 126n2
property, 18, 28, 137n14
Protestantism, 11, 20–22, 82, 121n16, 121n17, 121n19, 124n14. See also Weber, Max
psychoanalysis, x, 5–7, 14, 42, 49, 77–78, 117n1, 118n5; Freudian, 4–5, 59, 84, 118n7; Lacanian, 79–81, 84, 111, 118n7; post-Freudian, 1, 3, 5, 32, 54, 110, 124n13; schizoanalytic critique of, x, 60, 64, 67–68, 72, 75, 78–79, 125n1, 135n1
psychosis, 3, 33, 41–42, 46, 54
punitive projective identification, 48–49, 52–53, 123n7

qualities (primary/secondary), 15, 18, 88, 98, 100
quantities, x, 16–18, 58, 85–86, 90, 127n10, 1133n22; metric/non-metric, 87

realization: models of, 95, 133n22; of surplus value, 19, 28, 91, 114
recoding, 60, 74, 80. See also axiomatization; decoding
Reformation, Protestant. See Protestantism
Reich, Wilhelm, 5–6, 68, 110–111
repetition, 7–8, 42, 60, 78–79, 82–83, 113, 129n26
Rollerball. See Jewison, Norman
Russell, Bertrand, 87, 131n5, 131n6

Sade, Marquis de, x, 1–3 passim, 9, 18–21 passim, 32, 107, 117n2; novels, 11–15 passim, 26–27, 41, 65, 117n3, 118n5, 118n6, 118n3
Sadism, ix, 1–3, 8–9, 26–27, 32, 79, 107, 118n7, 133n21; and capitalist production, 13–14, 18–21, 84, 95, 113, 115, 137n14
Sartre, Jean-Paul, x, 60; *Nausea*, 34–35, 43–44
Savagery, 59, 67, 71–72, 83, 98
schizoanalysis, x, 59–61, 67–69, 79–83, 102, 107–109, 125n1, 125n2
schizophrenia, 33–35, 38–39, 74; schizoanalytic concept of, 61, 64, 78–80, 102, 105, 128n20, 128n22

science, 80, 96; axioms of, 61, 91, 97–99, 108, 133n23, 133n27; early modern, 15–16, 18; compared to philosophy, 63–64, 125n7
Specialization. *See* division of labor
Splitting, psychic. *See* borderline conditions
state, 70–71, 75, 133n22; axioms, 95–96, 100, 103, 112; banks, 16–17, 92, 96–97, 119n7; form of thought, 98–99, 127n11
Stranger, The. See Camus, Albert
Strozier, Charles, 51–52. *See also* supremacism, Christian
super-ego, 5, 79, 110, 112, 136n3; in borderline conditions, 41, 43–44, 47–49, 51–53, 56; in Lacan, 82–83, 111, 130n28; in Masochism, 27, 32; in Sadism, 14, 27, 32
supremacism: Aryan, 50–51; borderline, 47–50, 102, 109, 114, 124n12; Christian, 51–52; populist, 53, 109, 115, 124n12; white, 51, 124n12, 130n27

Theweleit, Klaus, 50, 60

Things. See Perec, Georges

utopia, 12–13, 85, 101, 111, 116
Utopia. See More, Thomas

value: abstract, 19, 97, 114; exchange, 16, 25, 50, 56, 89–90, 104; surplus, 6, 18–19, 28, 71, 75–77, 85–87, 90–91, 95, 96–97, 107, 110–111, 114; use, 16, 50, 56, 83; virtual 89, 93, 95. *See also* accumulation

wage slavery, 68, 105, 119n6
wealth, 5, 7, 19, 21, 24, 68, 90, 104, 120n10, 124n11; enjoyment of, 6, 19, 74, 77, 79, 85–86, 113–114, 130n1; liquid, 59, 77, 87, 91, 97–98
Weber, Max, 23; forms of rationality, 11, 77, 109; Protestantism, 11, 20–22, 121n16, 121n17, 121n19, 124n14
Wright, Richard, 48

Zimbardo, Philip, 4–5, 33

www.ingramcontent.com/pod-product-compliance
Lightning Source LLC
Chambersburg PA
CBHW031402230426
43670CB00006B/621